THE RAG DOLL

From Plain to Fancy

This book belongs to:

by elinor peace bailey

Editing and production direction by Mary Coyne Penders.
Technical editing by Lenore Parham.
Cover and book design by Linda Ray Lindeborg.
Production and Project Management by Character Place, Inc., Atlanta.
Dolls and illustrations by Elinor Peace Bailey.
Photography by Isaac Bailey; additional photography by Ames Photographic Illustration.
Chairs in photographs by Pat Wallace and Judy Schmitz.
Printing and color separation in Hong Kong by Regent Publishing Services Limited.

First edition.

Library of Congress Cataloging-in-Publication Data

Bailey, Elinor Peace
        The Rag Doll From Plain To Fancy.

        Bibliography: p.
        1. Rag Dolls   2. Dollmaking   3. Doll Clothes   4. Textile Crafts
TXu 630-430   1994
ISBN 1-881588-09-2

Quilt House Publishing
95 Mayhill Street
Saddle Brook, NJ 07662

Dedication

This book is dedicated to all my teachers, who pretend to be my students.

Acknowledgements

Special thanks to my editor, Mary Coyne Penders, for her exceptional dedication to our work, and to EZ International's Joe Mishkin and Charles Sabosik, who share my vision of what dolls can be. Books don't happen without family and friends. Thanks to them all, especially my husband Gary and my son Isaac, with whom it was my privilege to work. Thanks to Hani Stempler for answers to endless questions. Thanks to Miriam Gourley, author of *Cloth Dolls. How To Make Them*, for consultation and encouragement, and to Jamie Draluck for advice about photography. Thanks always to my Sally.

Preface

Twelve years of traveling throughout the country to teach dollmaking has given me an appreciation for what is possible when people find out they can make something for no reason other than revealing their own fantasies. I watch as my students drop their heavy responsibilities at the door and come to play with me.

Some are gifted seamstresses and some are novices, but all are looking for one thing. They are searching for a piece of themselves, a small mirror of who they are on that particular day.

In most of the classes that I teach, we use one of several patterns that I have designed, which range from simple to outrageous. Students enjoy the challenge of making choices with fabrics and trims to bring each doll closer to individual expression. I imagine that as you go through the projects in this book you'll discover that the process is great fun.

The Rag Doll From Plain To Fancy may be read on three levels. First, there is the story of the struggle between the doll and the dollmaker, which may be a familiar one to you. You won't be the first to report that you have wrestled with making a doll who insisted on being nothing at all like you had in mind!

Second, if you have always wanted to make a doll that was uniquely your own, you can consider my approach to the challenge. In order to write this book, I needed to know how to make each doll, and then tell you how you can make them. As I went from one stage to the next, I was impressed by how much I learned from going through the entire process and writing it all down. Through the process of telling you how to do it, I informed myself. This will happen to you when you read my account of the process.

Third, for those who wish to make the dolls as they are presented in the book, you will find full-sized patterns to guide you. I've included complete instructions and hints about techniques which may improve your skills.

The Rag Doll From Plain To Fancy may be used as a classroom text for dollmaking classes. Each chapter may be subdivided to provide at least two class sessions, taking a student from simple to more advanced constructions. The finished dolls provide the incentive for going through the entire design process. It is worthwhile to encourage students to design and make their own dolls, based on the techniques presented in this book.

Whether you want to be entertained by the doll's story, or to create your own original dolls, or to make the dolls in the book, I know you will enjoy becoming a member of the doll community. I think you will also be entertained by what is presented here.

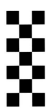

Table Of Contents

Supplies, Sources & Patterns

Here is a general list of supplies needed to make rag dolls. Included are the sources for some of the products I like to use. In each chapter you will find particular supply lists for each doll, including fabric requirements.

SUPPLIES

- Scissors for both paper and fabric
- Pencil
- Ruler or tape measure
- Template plastic
- Very fine marking pens, black and brown
- Ultra fine point permanent marker by Sharpie.®
- Brush-tip marking pens: Y&C PermaWriter II and Y&C FabricMate by Yasumoto
- Crayola crayons
- Dizzle Tints
- Gluestick
- Tacky craft glue
- Stop Fraying™ by Aleene's Glue
- Dollmaker's needles, #3 and #5
- Sharps or other hand-sewing needles
- Size 7 and sizes 14-18 yarn darners
- Quilting thread

- Waxed linen thread or crochet string
- Pearl cotton embroidery thread
- Bow Whip Turning Tool by Specialty Distributors, Post Office Box 19, Logan, Utah 84321.
- Stuffing Fork by Barbara Willis Designs, 415 Palo Alto Ave., Mountain View, CA 94041.
- Wok stick or chopstick
- Craft sticks (popsicle sticks)
- Poly-fil® stuffing by Fairfield Processing Corporation
- Small design board of foam core

PATTERNS

Patterns for the dolls and their clothes are located at the end of each chapter. Each pattern includes a seam allowance, indicated by the dotted line that is also the stitching line. Notice that I use a narrow seam allowance for both the dolls and the clothing. Each pattern shape is marked with the number of pieces you need to cut. Appliqué placement is indicated on the pattern. Drawings for the faces are included in each pattern section. If you'd like to change any of the patterns, let your imagination be your guide.

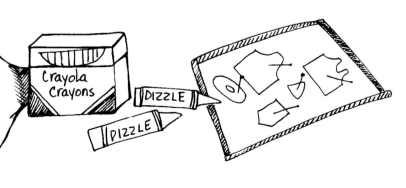

Your Sewing Machine

Let's talk about sewing machines. You'll be using your machine a lot to make these dolls, and there are very important considerations when you are investing your time and resources.

If you are lucky, your sewing machine is your best friend. You clean it once a year, and oil it when necessary. You know how to clean out the dust bunnies and you treat your machine with respect. You know that you must change your needle after each eight hours of sewing. You know that when your machine acts up, you first re-thread it, and then inspect the needle to see if it is in backwards, because that is usually the problem. You never ever use cheap thread out of one of those infamous sale baskets because this kind of thread throws off the tension, and that is the last thing you need.

Being a traveling crafter is "in" these days, which means that it is not "in" to be unable to get your machine to class, or to get your machine out of its cabinet. Use a luggage carrier to save aggravation, and practice unpacking your machine.

If you have been burdened by a lesser quality or aged machine, purchased because "I don't sew enough to justify the expense," or because a well-meaning mate remembers what his mother used, "was good enough for Mama..." well, not any more!

I urge you to inspect the family "toys." Add up the investment in tools, computers, electronics, cars, boats and time spent in front of television (time is money, you know). Compare. If you don't see an equitable situation, then make adjustments. Buy yourself a good machine, friend. You'll never regret it.

Comparison shop. You should be able to lift your machine. You should love your dealer because your dealer will be maintaining, repairing and instructing you on how to use your machine. You should be able to take your machine to class with you and be happy with its performance there.

Most of all, your machine should be able to do what you want it to do. If you need to be stitching on canvas or leather, it should do that. Or if you wish to stitch on satin, silk and chiffon, your machine should be there for you. Don't overlook the possibility of a good used machine. Just make sure that the machine you choose will be a friend and not an enemy. Now let's move on to making dolls!

In The Beginning

The Doll's Story

The dollmaker sat her large self down in a comfortable chair and began to make a rag doll. Because the doll was intended as an infant's chewable, the pattern required little imagination. She cut the doll's body from a basic shape that resembled a gingerbread man, and then gave it a pancake construction. The bright color of the material breathed life into the doll, and that was all she needed to become serviceable.

"This is hardly my life's ambition," confided the doll, who resigned herself to a short, messy existence in the hands of a tiny master. She knew it was her fate to fade and rend in constant washings and tumble-drys.

"One day," the doll mused, "I will be buried in a toy box. What a sad fate for someone with my ambitions!" She dreamed of an incarnation as a more elegant creature, one who would work far less and even enjoy a bit of leisure.

The Dollmaker's Workshop

Making a doll can be as simple as finding a stick that imagination makes human. Or it may be so elaborate and technically demanding that even the most adventuresome craftsperson is intimidated.

We're going to avoid intimidation by starting at the beginning, which is usually a wise decision for the more prudent among us. Those of you who can't resist jumping into the process at the middle may start any place you like. I am giving you a simple, uncomplicated outline of a human form for making a basic rag doll. The pattern is located at the end of this chapter.

If you wish to start with your own drawing instead, whip out a blank sheet of paper and draw away. Remember that your pattern needs to include a scant 1/4" seam allowance if you are using a woven cotton fabric, unless the doll is very small or very large.

Very small dolls can be sewn first and then cut out. Use the pattern as a template, and sew 1/8" inside the line. Use a small stitch (1.5 on your sewing machine) and Stop-Fraying™ (by Aleene's Glue) to reinforce your seam. Stop-Fraying™ is an acrylic lacquer that will dry soft and keep your edges from fraying. This method is good for fingers, toes, and other tiny shapes.

Making a doll can be as simple as finding a stick that imagination makes human.

On a standard size doll, always double-stitch the seams to insure that the seam will not pull out. Make sure that you look at both sides to be certain that you have caught each seam successfully. Nothing is more irritating than turning a piece and finding that you haven't caught the seam.

Decrease the seam allowance when you are sewing around details such as a nose or fingers. Just a bit of a slip may mean a missing feature. Dolls resent things like that, you know, so pay attention. Practice counts! If you need a bit of extra help, use tiny pencil marks to indicate your stitch line. For those of us with "middle-aged" eyes, strong light helps; and, if you need them, find your glasses and wear them!

The fabric you select makes the doll wonderful. Pick something that pleases the "kid" in you. The first voice you hear will be hers.

If you are a beginning dollmaker, it is wise to avoid any problems that you can't solve. For example, use 100% cotton. Those fancy fabrics that slip and fray and shed are calculated to make you crazy. Remember that people who use those materials successfully have been at it a long time, and they are no doubt very clever and have a maid and no children. Just stick to the basics.

SUPPLIES
The Rag Doll

- 1/4 yard of cotton print for the body

- A scrap of flesh-colored fabric

- 2 yards of four-ply knitting yarn

- Poly-fil stuffing

- Size 14-18 yarn darning needle

- The Bow Whip turning tool

- Tapered bamboo stuffing tool (wok-stick or chopstick)

- Fine-tipped permanent marking pen (Sharpie pen)

- Very fine brown permanent marking pen (Pigma 0.1)

- Brush-tipped marking pens

- Stop-Fraying by Aleene's Glue

- A large box of Crayola crayons

- Plastic tints with glitter

- White plastic tee-shirt paint

- Fabric glue-stick

- Lightweight template plastic

DIRECTIONS

1. Trace the pattern onto lightweight pattern plastic, using a fine-tipped Sharpie pen. The solid line is your cutting line, and the broken line is your stitch line. If you punch a hole through each piece of plastic, and put your pattern pieces onto a notebook ring, they can be hung on a peg board in your craft room, if you are lucky enough to have one.

This is easy and you'll be done in a matter of minutes. The challenge lies in picking out the cotton fabric to make the doll. Remember that this is a doll, and a very simple one, so the fabric you select makes it wonderful. Just pick something that pleases the "kid" in you. The first voice you hear in your head will be hers.

2. Place selected fabrics with the right sides together. Lay the pattern on top of the fabric. Pin the pattern in place and cut. Use your good scissors, not those the kids use for cutting paper. You know the ones I mean, the scissors you hide under the mattress.

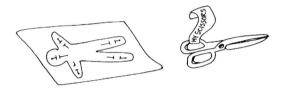

3. Select a bit of flesh-colored fabric that reflects one of the many colors found on real people, or choose a color you've conjured up in you head. Using the pattern, cut out the face.

4. Place the face on the front of the body, as indicated on the pattern. Use a fabric glue-stick to hold the face on the body, and then stay-stitch (straight-stitch) the face in place. Use a satin zig-zag stitch to cover the raw edges. Whether or not you are going to paint the face, at this stage it will be blank.

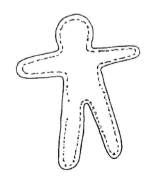

5. After the face fabric is in place, put the right sides of the body pieces together and stitch up the doll. Use a double row of stitches (one on top of the other), and leave the body seam open as indicated on the pattern piece.

6. Turn the doll right-side-out with the Bow Whip turning tool. Insert the tube into the casing, all the way to the tip of the arm or the leg. Push the dowel into the tip of the tube from the outside of the casing, and pull the fabric back over the dowel.

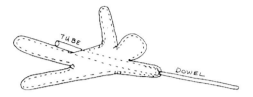

7. Stuffing is as important to a doll as batting is to a quilt. Sloppy or half-hearted stuffing may lead to a depressed doll, a very sorry sight, so you will want to stuff the doll with a good grade of stuffing. I suggest a stuffing with fibers that have been exploded in several directions, resulting in a random arrangement. Check several different brands in order to make a selection that suits you. I use Fairfield poly-fil. Your choices range from cotton balls in medicine bottles (or anything that feels the same) which stuffs like old oatmeal, to fine, silky, fluffy stuff that slips out of every crevice you put it in. Long fibers make a hard-edged finish which appeals to some dollmakers. I prefer fibers that lie in a random arrangement because they give a firm but responsive feel.

Students often ask me about the secret of stuffing. Trust me: there is no secret being hoarded by a group of select dollmakers. We are willing to share. The formula is: small pieces in small places. If you try to force too large a piece into a tiny channel, you will cause nasal congestion. No matter what you do, you will be unable to dislodge that wad. Nothing short of taking it out and beginning again will remedy this kind of mess. This doll should be filled, but left a bit soft so that she may be squeezed and enjoyed.

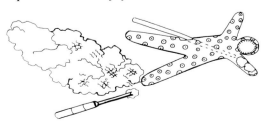

Half-hearted stuffing may lead to a depressed doll, so you will want to stuff the doll with a good grade of stuffing.

The stuffing formula: small pieces in small places.

11

8. Stitch the opening closed by hand, using tiny overcast stitches. If you're six years old, and you're helping Mom with this project, maybe she should do the final stitching.

9. If you are going to draw the face, wait until you have stuffed the body. Then you will have a taut canvas. Use a fine-tipped brown permanent marking pen that is suitable for fabric. You may also copy one of the faces I have drawn.

Choices, choices, choices, don't you hate them! First use a pencil and make a light line. Then, with a fine-tipped permanent marking pen, draw the face. Other options include brush-tipped pens suitable for fabric, crayons, plastic tints with glitter in them, and white plastic tee-shirt paint for the highlights. This is how I did mine.

10. Buttons and snaps make dandy eyes and noses. Do not use them, however, unless the child using the doll is beyond the chewing stage. Secure the buttons and snaps with care.

11. Use your fine-tipped permanent marking pen to draw a mouth. Or try drawing a face on felt or polyester suede. After you've experimented with my silly suggestions, try making a face that reflects your own fertile imagination.

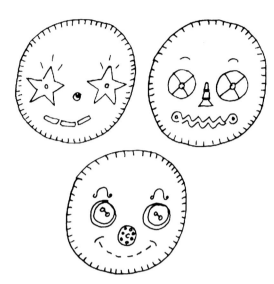

12. To make the doll's hair, use durable material like four-ply knitting yarn. Use a size 14-18 yarn darning needle with a sharp point, a long shank and a large eye. The needle must be big enough to lead the yarn through the head without a lot of pulling and tugging. Enter the doll's head by placing the needle at the back of the head. Pull the yarn through the head to the seam where an ear would be. Do not use a knot.

13. Make a small stay stitch to anchor the yarn. Make an overcast stitch over the seam to form a loop. Make another overcast stitch and pull it tight. Follow with another loop, and then a tight stitch, until you have make a row of stitches over the seam on the head from ear to ear. After the last tight stitch, bury the yarn and cut it off.

Improvisations

You can shrink this pattern at your photo-copy store and wear the small version, or blow it up and frighten people. In addition, here are some alternative patterns with a few new things to try your patience. All of them are simple improvisations on a five-pointed body. The CHICKEN DOLL is a whimsical addition to every child's doll collection. The SILLY WEARABLE, attached to a garment, proclaims that dolls belong to all ages, sometimes just for fun.

SUPPLIES

The Chicken Doll

- 1/4 yard of yellow for the body of the chicken

- Scraps of red-orange for beak and comb

- Orange for feather ruff

- Scraps of blue or green felt for star feet

- Two buttons for eyes

DIRECTIONS

1. Appliqué the contrasting ruff of feathers on the head, using a stay-stitch and a satin zig-zag to cover the raw edges.

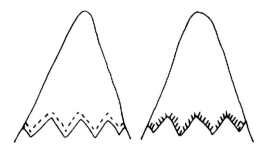

2. Stitch the beak. Turn and stuff lightly.

3. Top-stitch an opening for the beak, using a contrasting thread. Stitch the beak as indicated, so that it will fit into the seam.

4. Placing the right sides together, stitch the chicken. Leave an opening as indicated on the pattern.

5. Clip, turn and lightly stuff the wings.

6. Top-stitch the wings with large, contrasting zig-zag stitches to form feathers.

7. Finish stuffing the wing and the rest of the doll. Then close the opening by hand with overcast stitches.

8. With right sides together, stitch up the comb. Turn, stuff, and close by hand. Tack in place on the head as shown.

9. Use buttons for eyes. Sew firmly in place.

10. Using the pattern, cut out two stars from felt or polyester suede, and attach.

Shrink this pattern (photo-copy) and wear the small version, or blow it up and frighten people.

SUPPLIES

Silly Wearable Doll

- 1/4 yard for body of doll

- Scraps for face, hat brim, feather and hair

- Two 5/8" buttons for the doll's feet

- Two 1/4" buttons for front of doll

DIRECTIONS

1. Using your plastic pattern and selected fabric, cut out the wearable body. Placing the right sides together, stitch around the body, leaving open where indicated.

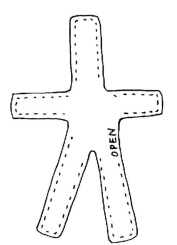

2. Clip, turn and stuff. Close by hand with an overcast stitch.

3. Cut the face from flesh-colored fabric. With the right sides together, stitch around the face. Make a slash at the back for turning. Turn and press. Tack in place as indicated.

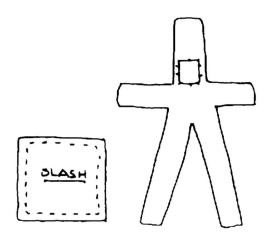

4. Copy the drawing of the face with a fine-tipped permanent marking pen, brush tipped pens, crayons and tints.

5. Cut out the brim of the hat. Use the brim pattern to cut an inner-lining of batting.

6. Place the right sides of the hat brim fabrics together, and place the batting on top. Stitch around the brim through the fabric and the batting.

7. Turn right-side-out from the opening at the center.

14

8. Slip over the crown of the hat, just above the face. Cover the raw edges with a bit of ribbon.

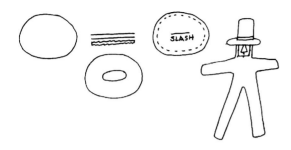

9. Cut the feather, using four layers of fabric.

10. Fold the feather in half and stitch along the fold. Clip the opposite edge to make feathers.

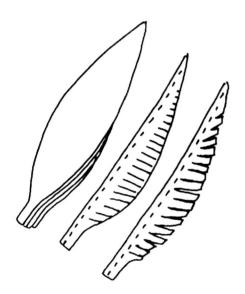

11. Tack the feather in place to trim the hat.

12. Make the hair from two layers of fabric measuring 2" x 5". Fold the fabric rectangle in half; fold in half again.

13. Make a row of stitches along the edge. Clip the opposite edge to make hair.

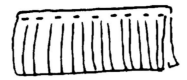

14. Wrap the hair around the back of the face and tack in place.

15. Add the buttons, and wear the doll on your jacket. People will talk to you, even if they never have before. If you have ever felt ignored, a wearable doll will put an end to that situation.

Wear the doll on your jacket. If you have ever felt ignored, a wearable doll will put an end to that situation.

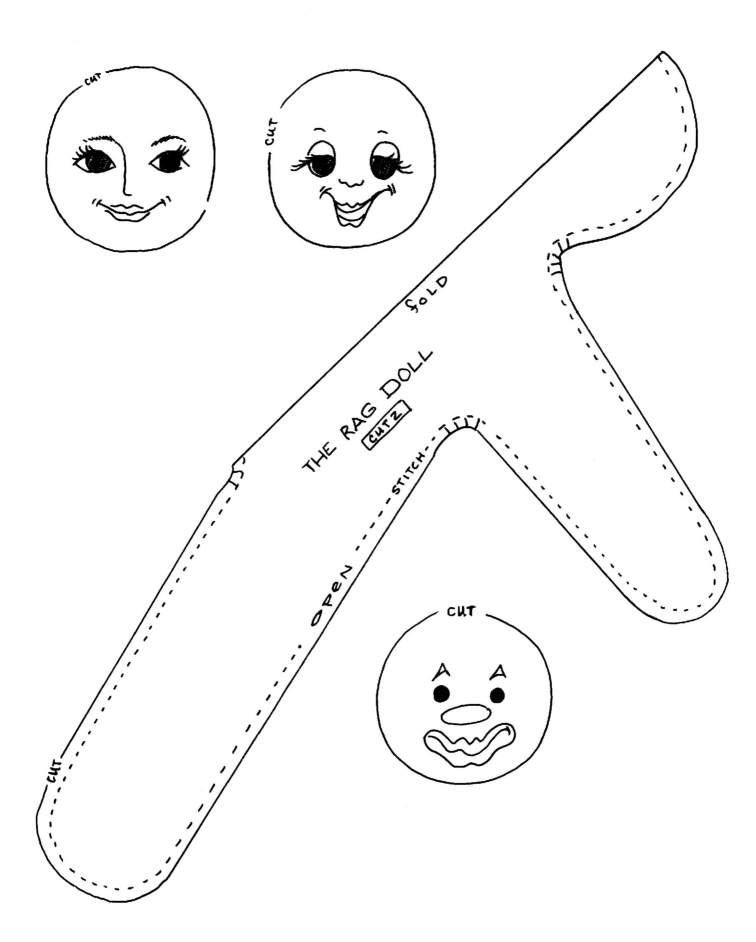

FOLD

THE RAG DOLL

CUT2

OPEN — — — — — — STITCH — — — —

CUT

CUT

CUT

CUT

CUT

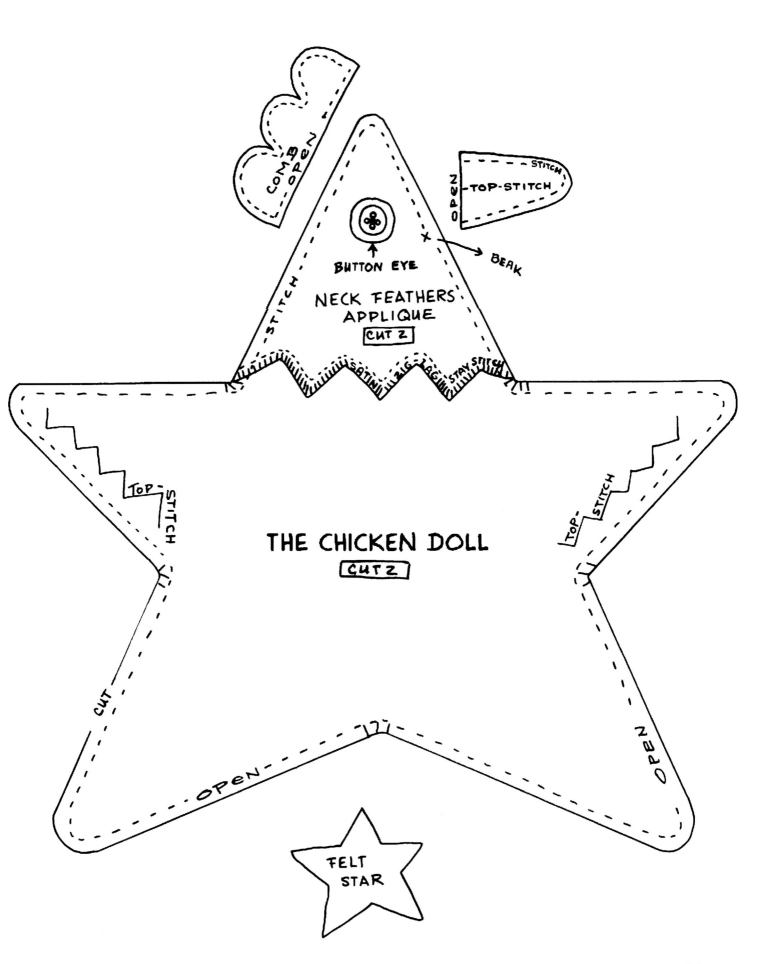

COMB OPEN

TOP-STITCH

OPEN

STITCH

BUTTON EYE

BEAK

x

NECK FEATHERS
APPLIQUE

CUT 2

STITCH

SATIN ZIG ZAG STAY STITCH

TOP-STITCH

TOP-STITCH

THE CHICKEN DOLL

CUT 2

CUT

OPEN

OPEN

FELT
STAR

17

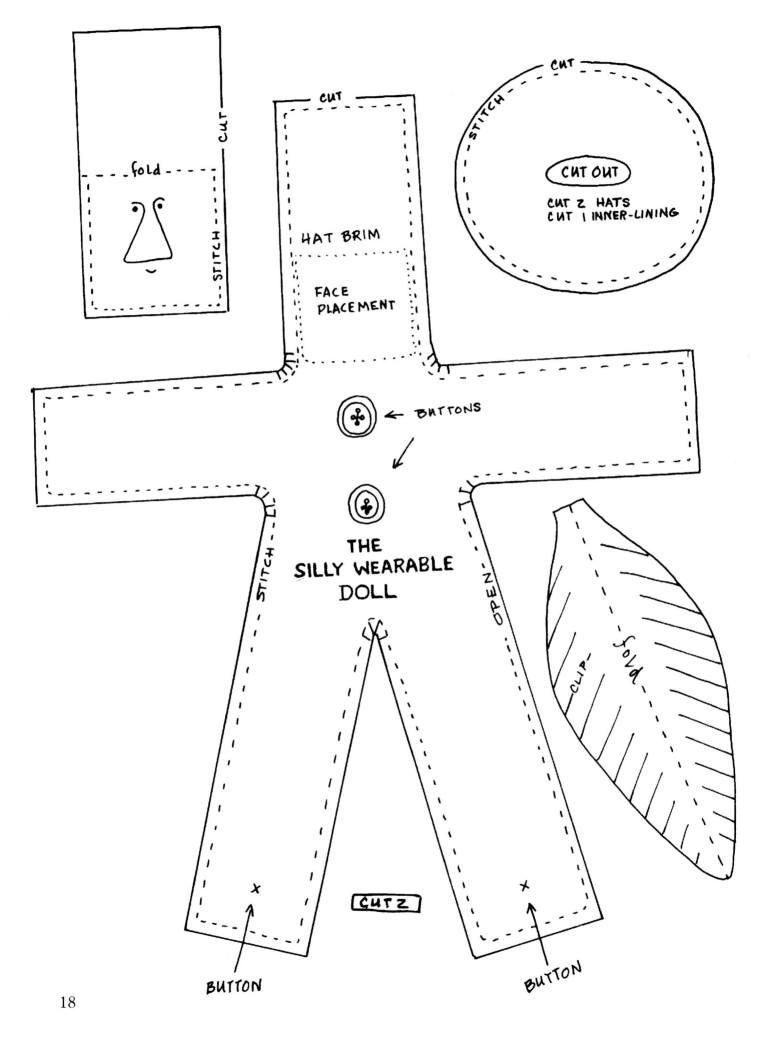

fold

CUT

STITCH

CUT

HAT BRIM

FACE PLACEMENT

CUT

STITCH

CUT OUT

CUT 2 HATS
CUT 1 INNER-LINING

← BUTTONS

STITCH

OPEN

CLIP

fold

**THE
SILLY WEARABLE
DOLL**

X

X

CUT 2

BUTTON

BUTTON

18

Clothes Make The Doll

The Doll's Story

The dollmaker shifted her position and considered this simple rag doll. Well loved and frayed, the doll begged for new life.

"What if," mused the dollmaker, "we add clothes?"

"Clothes!" snapped the doll. "Oh yes, clothes. The child would take them off, put them on, lose them, abuse them. Sure, she loves doll clothes."

"But the child is older now," the dollmaker pointed out. "Maybe she would be like the children in old story books and wash out her tiny doll clothes, mend them and stitch up some more."

"You're dreaming," said the doll, her tone definitely sarcastic.

The dollmaker thought for a bit. "You're going to need hands and feet, you know," she said.

"Fingers? Are you going to give me fingers?" cried the doll.

The dollmaker smiled indulgently. "No, let's start simply, and give you mitten hands."

"A mitten hand? If I had fingers I could tweak your nose.'

"And I could leave you as you are," warned the dollmaker, which put an end to the chatter.

The dollmaker began fingering some bright colored cloth that she found in her stash. The colors were striped in many shades across a single piece of fabric. Just looking at all the different colors excited her. She began to imagine what she could do if she used a different color or shade for each bit of the doll's clothing. The doll watched the excitement reflected in the dollmaker's face. She had seen it before, whenever the dollmaker began to play with color.

"What are you thinking?" demanded the doll impatiently. "Here I am, hardly fit to look at, and you're daydreaming."

"Daydreaming," pronounced the dollmaker, "is part of being creative. Without daydreaming, nothing interesting would ever happen. Dolls would be the very first thing to be eliminated if it weren't for daydreaming."

The doll reflected a moment and sighed. "At some point we need to get to work here. All this visionary stuff isn't going to change a thing, and without some sort of change I'm fit for garbage."

The dollmaker looked sympathetically at the doll, who really did need some attention. She began.

The Dollmaker's Workshop

You can add hands and feet fairly easily to your original pattern. But first check the proportions. What worked for the pancake (basic doll) shape may or may not hold up as the doll becomes more realistic. The arms need to come from the fingertip to the mid-thigh. You can stand up and look in the mirror to test this theory.

We still want to create a play doll, so let's stick to the image of a child. You can make this doll into a little boy by just adding ears. Somehow ears always make boys.

"Daydreaming is part of being creative. Dolls would be the very first thing to be eliminated if it weren't for daydreaming."

You can make this doll into a little boy by just adding ears. Somehow ears always make boys.

Remember, all appliqués must first be secured with a straight stitch or stay-stitch.

Making Hands, Feet and Underwear

1. A mitten hand is easy to construct. Look at your own hand to draw an outline.

2. Now, simplify that hand.

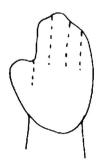

3. For the feet, the simplest approach is to draw them pointing away from the body.

4. Let's make shoes. For this doll, the socks and the shoes will be applied to the feet. Draw them as you would on a paper doll, only this time the doll is stuffed.

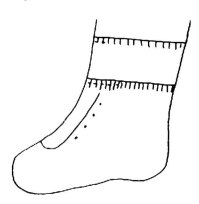

5. If you draw the body of the doll with simple details, you can clothe it by adding appliqués (one surface of fabric applied to another). Use the pattern to cut out the underwear, shoes and socks as you would see them on a paper doll. They should fit to the form of the doll's body, both back and front, and your doll will then be partially clothed.

6. With your fine-tipped permanent marking pen you can draw some additional details on the clothing.

The Doll's Story

The doll approved. "I like the underwear idea. That way I'm never naked. I hate being cold and uncomfortable."

"And it frees me from considerable guilt," sighed the dollmaker. "I have to dress all the dolls. I can't just leave them there without any clothes."

"I should think not!" exclaimed the doll.

"Shall we continue?" asked the dollmaker.

"Continue," replied the doll.

The Dollmaker's Workshop

Appliquéing clothing to a doll body gives the illusion of something very elaborate without the work of designing clothes that fit. But remember, all appliqués must first be secured with a straight stitch or stay-stitch. The raw edges can then be finished with a satin zig-zag stitch. The satin stitch is not a structural stitch; it does not necessarily hold things together.

Enlarging Your Pattern

When you purchase a pattern or design one yourself that needs to be enlarged, you can take it to your local quick print shop. It's fun to play at the printer's, but be advised that sometimes it works and sometimes it doesn't. When I took the little doll pattern that I designed to my local printer, I thought I could blow it up by twenty-five percent with no risk to the proportions.

What I found was that the doll lost something in the translation. I had to add a full inch of height at the waist in order to keep the five and one-half heads of height needed for the child doll I had in mind.

Realistic adult dolls measure about seven heads. Sometimes we exaggerate the height of the doll to make it appear more elegant. Fashion designers use this technique, and so do expressive painters. So check for distortion when you enlarge a pattern at the print shop. It can be corrected if you are careful.

The doll pattern that I took to the printer needed to be adjusted for the changes that occurred. The clothing seemed to work without adjustment.

DIRECTIONS
Making Clothes For The Rag Doll

Making clothing is less difficult than it might appear. It is a process that requires more trial and error than the careful measuring you would use if you were designing clothes for a person. If you have followed my ideas for designing your own doll body pattern, you have a major advan-

tage. You can lay that pattern out and draw around it, adding seam allowances. Or you can use the pattern for the *Small Doll* at

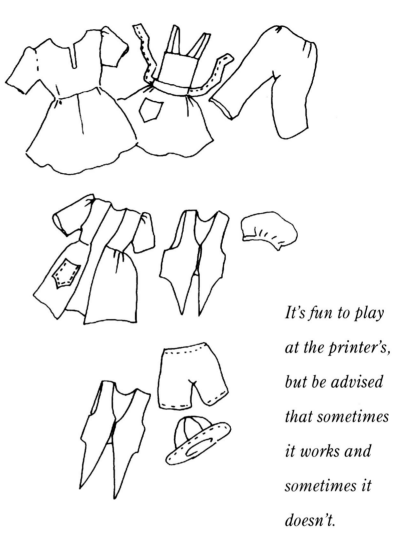

It's fun to play at the printer's, but be advised that sometimes it works and sometimes it doesn't.

the end of this chapter. If the doll is essentially one of "pancake" construction (just two flat sides), you won't have to deal with darts.

We'll start with knickers. Knickers are a nice touch if she is tumbling about. A girl can never be too careful, you know.

1. If you are designing a pair of knickers to go on a doll with a pancake (basic doll) construction, lay the pattern on a piece of paper, allowing for fullness at the waist to make gathers, and allowing enough height for a casing for 1/4" elastic.

2. Then draw a simple crotch, and label the pattern piece with a note to cut two fabric pieces.

Knickers are a nice touch if she is tumbling about. A girl can never be too careful, you know.

When you are designing, be sure and leave a paper trail of your work. This record allows you to make changes and alterations.

The knickers can become long pants for the *Large Doll* we're going to make. They can be enlarged at the copy center. I enlarged them 25% and then made them longer.

Now let's consider a dress for the *Small Doll*. Some familiarity with real people dress patterns, including the basic set-in sleeve and arm hole, is helpful. This is what the basic sleeve and bodice look like.

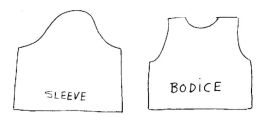

3. Try laying the doll pattern on a piece of paper and draw lines along the top of the shoulder and the side of the body. Add a scant 1/4" seam allowance at the shoulder and maybe a bit more at the side under the arm.

4. Take the doll pattern off the paper and fill in a neckline and a waist. Make a curved line from the shoulder to just under the arm, and there you have a bodice.

The easiest way to finish a neck, and create an opening at the back of the neck to get the doll in and out of her dress, is to make facings. It sounds scary, but it's a lot less tedious than itsy bitsy hems or, worse yet, bindings.

5. Once the basic top fits the way you like, lay the pattern pieces under a piece of paper and trace the facings. The facing will go all the way down the bodice for a coat, and the bodice and the facing will be left completely open.

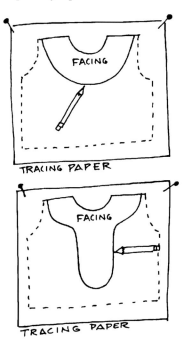

6. Consider this drawing of the sleeve. The hump at the top allows for fullness at the cap of the sleeve. You can eliminate most of the gathers for a boy's shirt because it should lie flat. There is a point at which the hump can be too large for the armhole, but you can experiment until the size is right. I usually eyeball the sleeve and ease it in; it must fit in the armhole shape.

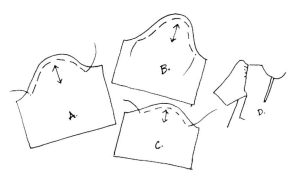

7. The length and the fullness of the skirt should be determined by the maker. I have loved putting very full skirts on tiny waists. After all, when you're in control, you're in control. Just stitch up the side seam of the gathered skirt and stitch it into the bodice. When the dress is used as a coat on the *Large Doll*, the skirt is left open, and faced with an inch or so of its own width.

8. The little vest is taken from Sally Lampi's *"Long and Lean Vest"* pattern, and made much smaller. When I make it for myself, I make it much larger. A little piece like this is easier to do if it is fully lined. In turning this vest and lining, I took a cue from a vest pattern designed by Virginia Robertson of the *Osage County Quilt Factory*. As we go through the process in the pattern, you'll see what I mean. Designing something is one thing; constructing it may be quite another.

9. The bib apron is easy. The bib needs to be totally lined, and should reveal at least a bit of the dress. This doll will have layers of clothes. The ties could be ribbon, but if this is a play doll, fabric ties will last longer.

10. Finally, here is a hat made with a curved triangle shape, repeated four times. Four triangles with curved edges form the crown of the hat. The brim is simply a donut that you slip over the crown and attach.

Again, trial and error is still the best teacher. Remember to keep a paper trail of your experiments. This will help you with future designing.

The Doll's Story

"All right. Enough of this!" exclaimed the frayed, worn out rag doll. "I am in need of repair, and all this preparation and talk is getting us nowhere."

So the dollmaker got out her scissors and began to cut.

The Dollmaker's Workshop

SUPPLIES

Doll Bodies And Clothing

- 1/8 to 1/4 yard scraps of solid color pieces of cotton fabric for the clothes and the body. Include the following:

- Fabrics for the doll bodies

Remember to keep a paper trail of your experiments. This will help you with future designing.

- Fabric for the knickers for the small doll

- Fabric for the pants for the large doll

- *Three* colors, one for the sleeve, one for the bodice, and one for the skirt of the dress for the small doll

- *Two* colors for the upper and lower body of the coat for the large doll

- Assorted colors of fabric for the vest, vest lining, apron, hats for both dolls, and apron pocket

- Fabric for the turtleneck shirt for the larger doll

- Small pieces for appliqué underwear, socks, and shoes on both dolls

I used printed fabrics for the hat and the pocket on the coat for the larger doll. I count twenty solid colored fabrics and two printed fabrics for both dolls. If you can find Color Bars™ by Chapel House Fabrics for E-Z International, you will have an ample selection of solid colors from just a few half-yard cuts of fabric.

Flesh, you may have noticed, comes in many colors, from peach, beige, red and yellow-browns to dark, rich chocolate browns and black.

DIRECTIONS

Making The Doll Bodies

The following directions apply to both dolls.

1. Cut the dolls' bodies from flesh-colored fabric. Flesh, you may have noticed, comes in many colors, from peach, beige, red and yellow-browns to dark, rich chocolate browns and black. Consider your range of choices. They present us with a lot of creative freedom.

2. Working with the patterns at the end of the chapter, cut out clothing appliqués from the fabrics you have selected. Use the patterns in the interior of the doll's body pattern for appliquéd underwear for the smaller doll, and for the leotard for the larger doll. Use the patterns on the interior of the large and small leg patterns for the socks and the shoes. The details on the underwear for the smaller doll may be drawn with your fine-tipped permanent marking pen.

SMALL DOLL   LARGE DOLL

3. Using a fabric gluestick, dab on tiny bits of glue to hold the appliqués in place. The glue replaces pins, but does not replace stitching. Stay-stitch the appliqués in place, and then cover the raw edges with a satin zig-zag stitch. Set the stitch width at 2.5 and the length a little below 1/2.

SMALL DOLL   LARGE DOLL

4. Place the two sides of the small doll's body with right sides together, and stitch up the doll. Use scant 1/4" seams. Be careful; bumps and jags in your stitching will make a difference. Leave an opening as indicated on the pattern piece for turning. Follow the same process for making the body of the large doll.

5. Turn the body of the doll over and put another row of stitching on top of the last row. This enables you to see if you have secured every seam.

6. Clip each inward curve to the stitch line. Turn, and lightly stuff the hands.

7. Look at the pattern and top-stitch the fingers by machine. Start at the top of the little finger and back-tack. Stitch down to the tip of the finger, back-tack and jump the thread to the tip of the second finger. Continue until you've completed the hand, including the thumb line.

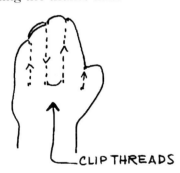

8. Stuff the remainder of the hand and arm, and top-stitch an arm joint. This allows the arm to swing stiffly back and forth. This construction is called a *stitched joint*. Needless to say, joints are a topic unto themselves. If you make these dolls in sequence, you will learn a few different approaches to jointing a doll.

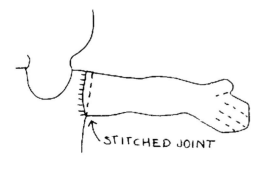

9. Stuff the legs, and make a stitched joint at the top of each leg.

10. Stuff the head and neck firmly. The neck is difficult to keep firm and stiff. Do not pound on the stuffing or it will lump. Put bits of stuffing in place and press firmly. It's like biscuit dough; mess with it as little as possible. Remember, don't stuff as if you were churning butter. Put little pieces in little places, and big pieces in big places. Try not to cause lumps by leaving pockets where there is no stuffing. Lumps are very ugly things.

11. Close the body by hand with tiny overcast stitches. Remember that these directions are the same for the second doll.

The Doll's Story

"Very ugly," glowered the doll, who was beginning to feel renewed by this incarnation and didn't welcome the idea of lumps.

She moved her arms stiffly to clap her hands together.

"Not bad," she said. "This is all very well, this clapping and so forth, but you know I am bald. This won't do. I assume you have a solution?"

"Oh, many," replied the dollmaker. "If you were a country doll we could give you some rag hair by tearing half-inch strips of fabric, putting the strips in bunches and tying them in knots. Then we would stitch them on your head."

"How quaint," smirked the doll. "I suppose you'd give me shoe-button eyes?"

"Of course," said the dollmaker.

"Oh, really." The doll was not amused.

"We could get some curly roving and make you a very romantic do," the dollmaker offered.

"I thought I was to be a play doll. Can you imagine what I'd look like after five minutes in the hands of a child? A mess!"

Stuffing is like biscuit dough; mess with it as little as possible.

The dollmaker admitted that was true. "So let's give you yarn braids; they're practical and perky."

"Oh, good grief...perky? All right," groaned the doll. "I suppose yarn braids will do."

The Dollmaker's Workshop

DIRECTIONS
Making Hair

1. Cut twenty-four 14" strands of 4-ply yarn for the small doll.

2. Lay the strands out and stitch across them several times at the center with the sewing machine. The stitching forms the part.

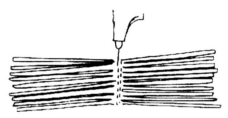

3. Match the hair at the part to the center of the head, and tack about 1/2" into the face, and 3/4" down the back of the head.

4. Stitch in place. Pull the yarn back to about where the ears would be if there were ears, and overcast a few stitches to hold the hair together.

5. Braid, and tie off the braids with pieces of yarn.

6. For hair on the larger doll, use the turkey stitch, the same stitch that was used on the basic rag doll. Use a size 14 yarn darning needle. Bring the needle through the head to the seam, where there would be an ear if there were one.

7. Overcast a stitch, and pull it tight. Overcast again, and leave a 1/2" loop. These tight stitches should be as close together as possible. Repeat this across the head. Then make another row for bangs, and two or three rows at the back of the head if you wish a full head of hair.

8. Finish by pulling yarn through a loop, pulling tight, and burying the yarn.

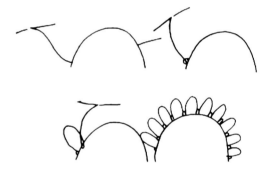

SUPPLIES
Making Faces

- Fine-tipped permanent marking pen

- Brush-tipped fabric pens

- Crayons of blue-based pink and brown-orange (if using Crayola crayons, box of 64, use Thistle and Bittersweet)

- Sparkling tints of peach and light blue

DIRECTIONS
Making Faces

1. Copy face in place with a very light pencil. Then use the fine-tipped pen to make the face permanent.

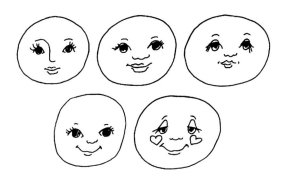

2. Use a brush-tipped fabric pen for a light sprinkling of freckles.

3. Draw the lips very softly to keep the doll child-like. Make the eyes soft and lightly shadowed.

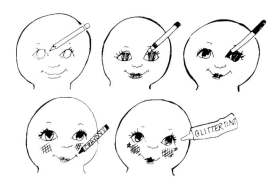

4. Use sparkling tints to complete the doll face and give it some glitter.

The Doll's Story

The doll looked in the mirror. She was beginning to feel quite restored. She shivered and demanded, "Could you get busy with the clothes?"

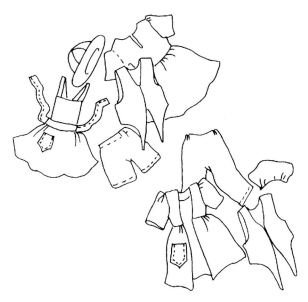

The Dollmaker's Workshop

DIRECTIONS
Making Doll Clothes

Knickers And Pants

1. Cut knickers or long pants from selected fabrics.

2. Stitch up side seams, crotch, and inseams.

3. Hem to suit, and make a casing by turning a tiny hem at the top, and then a 3/8" hem to receive a 1/4" elastic at the waist.

4. Stitch casing. Leave a 3/8" opening to guide elastic through. Use a tiny safety pin or bodkin. (Ha! Do you know what a bodkin is?)

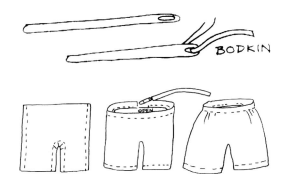

5. Stitch the elastic together and help the doll dress in the shorts or long pants. She puts them on one leg at a time.

DIRECTIONS
Dress For The Small Doll And Coat For The Large Doll

The dress and coat are made from the same pattern with slight variations. Don't you wish that making your own clothes were this simple?

1. Using the dress pattern, cut the following dress parts from selected fabrics. You can use a different color, and even printed fabric, for each part.
    a. bodice
    b. skirt, 4-1/2" x 18" for small doll
       6" x 22-1/2" for large doll
    c. sleeve
    d. front neck facing
    e. back neck facing

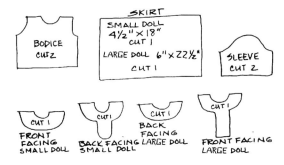

2. With right sides together, stitch shoulder seams of bodice and press.

3. With right sides together, stitch facings at shoulder.

4. Press a tiny hem around the outer edge of facing, and zig-zag the edge to finish.

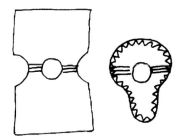

5. With right sides together, place the facing on top of the bodice, matching it at the neck to create an opening at the back. Pin in place, and carefully stitch to form the slash opening.

6. Make two stitches across the bottom of the back opening. Clip into the corners and around neck. Turn and press.

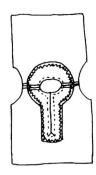

7. Gather the sleeve as indicated on pattern piece. Pull the gathers together and, with right sides together, ease sleeves into armhole.

8. Pin and stitch in place. Repeat for second sleeve.

9. There, you've got it. Clip, and with right sides together, stitch up side seams and sleeves.

10. Decide on the length of the sleeve, and hem the sleeve by hand. Don't whine! Handwork is good.

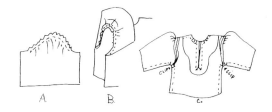

11. With right sides together, make a tube skirt.

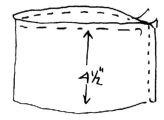

12. Gather the skirt to fit the bodice. Make sure that the seam is at the center back and, with right sides together, pin in place. Stitch.

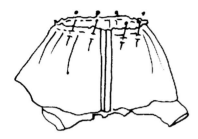

13. Turn, and finger press the seam up into the bodice. Top stitch the seam to make the skirt lie flat.

14. Hem to suit.

15. For button closure, use crochet string to form a chain stitch buttonhole loop. You can also use a snap or hook and eye.

16. Put the small doll in the dress and maybe she'll stop complaining.

DIRECTIONS
Coat For The Large Doll

1. Cut two bodice pieces. Then cut one bodice piece in half. With right sides together, stitch shoulder seams and press.

2. Cut two facings, using the facings marked for the coat. With right sides together, stitch facings at shoulder.

3. Press a tiny hem around the outer edge of the facing and zig- zag the edge to finish.

4. Stitch the facing to the bodice, leaving the bottom of the bodice open.

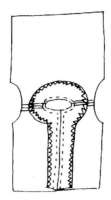

5. Follow dress instructions for sleeves and side seams.

6. Do not tube the skirt. Instead, hem the side seams and put them in front.

7. Gather the skirt. With right sides together, stitch the skirts to the bodice, making sure you include the facing.

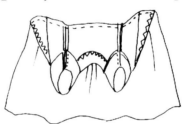

8. Press seams up, towards the bodice, and top stitch to make the skirting of the coat lie flat.

9. Fold in facings and press. Skirt will form a facing at the opening of the coat.

10. Hem to suit, and tack facings in place.

11. Cut out the fabric for the patch pocket on the front of the coat.

12. With right sides together, stitch around the patch pocket. Leave an opening at the side of the pocket to turn.

13. Turn with your Bow Whip, and press.

14. Top stitch the pocket in place on the right hand side of the front of the coat so that the doll can carry a hanky and some small change.

DIRECTIONS
Making Vests

1. Cut out vest and lining from selected fabrics.

2. With right sides together, stitch side seams of vest, and repeat for lining. Press.

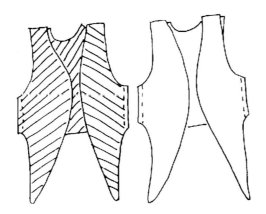

3. With right sides together, stitch lining to vest at front, back, neck and armholes, using 1/8" seams. Leave open at shoulders to turn.

4. Clip, and turn through armholes. This is not easy, but it is possible. Seams are 1/8". Smarten up, bunch!

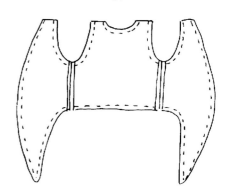

5. Press, and join the shoulders at the seams, front side of vest to front side.

6. Zig-zag to finish. Aw, come on, now. Don't drag out your serger. Hey, we're lookin' good!

DIRECTIONS
Apron For The Small Doll

1. Cut the apron pieces from selected fabrics. Include
    a. skirt 4" x 9"
    b. sash, cut two 2" x 7"
    c. top ties, cut two 1-1/2" x 8"
    d. apron belt, cut one
       1-1/2" x 3-1/2"
    e. apron bib, cut two
    f. pockets, cut two

2. Hem the side edges and the bottom of the apron skirt.

3. Gather the top of apron skirt.

4. With right side of the belt to wrong side of the apron skirt, fit the skirt to the belt. Turn in side edges of belt so they will be finished.

5. Turn the belt to the front of the apron to form a band. Leave the edges open to receive the apron sashes. Stitch in place.

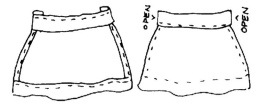

6. Make the patch pocket by putting right sides together. Stitch, leaving an opening at the side. Turn and press.

7. Top-stitch pocket on the skirt, so the doll can put her right hand in it.

8. With right sides together, fold the top ties and apron sashes lengthwise. Top stitch, leaving open at one end. Turn with the Bow Whip and press.

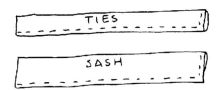

9. Crimp the open end of each sash, and insert into opening at side of belt. Top-stitch.

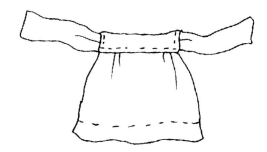

10. Make the bib of the apron by putting the right sides together and stitching around the bib. Leave an opening about 1/2" on a side to turn. Turn and press.

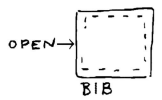

11. Tuck in raw edges, and stitch in place onto the apron skirt.

12. Tack the apron ties in place on the bib and tie onto the doll.

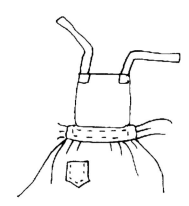

13. Stitch a button onto the dress to trim it.

DIRECTIONS

Making Hats

Hat #1 For Small Doll

1. Cut the following hat pieces from selected fabrics:
   a. brim - cut 2
   b. brim inner-lining of fleece - cut 1
   c. crown - cut 4

2. With right sides together, stitch two pieces of crown together. Repeat with remaining two pieces.

3. Stack the two pieces for the brim with right sides together. Place the inner lining of batting on the outside of one of the brims.

4. Stitch around the brim.

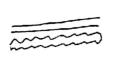

5. Slash the opening at the center of all three layers and press. Turn from slash.

6. Cut out opening circle that will fit over the doll's head.

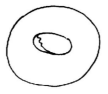

7. With right sides together, insert crown into brim. Stitch in place. There it is!

Hat #2 For Large Doll

1. Make a tube of a piece of fabric, 3" x 12".

2. Turn so that the seam is inside, and press in a hem at the bottom and top edges.

3. Gather the top edge. Place on the larger doll's head, pull the gathers and fasten. Give the hat a jaunty tilt.

4. If you want a hat to take on and off, then stitch a band on the bottom and plan to make two or three more when this one gets lost.

34

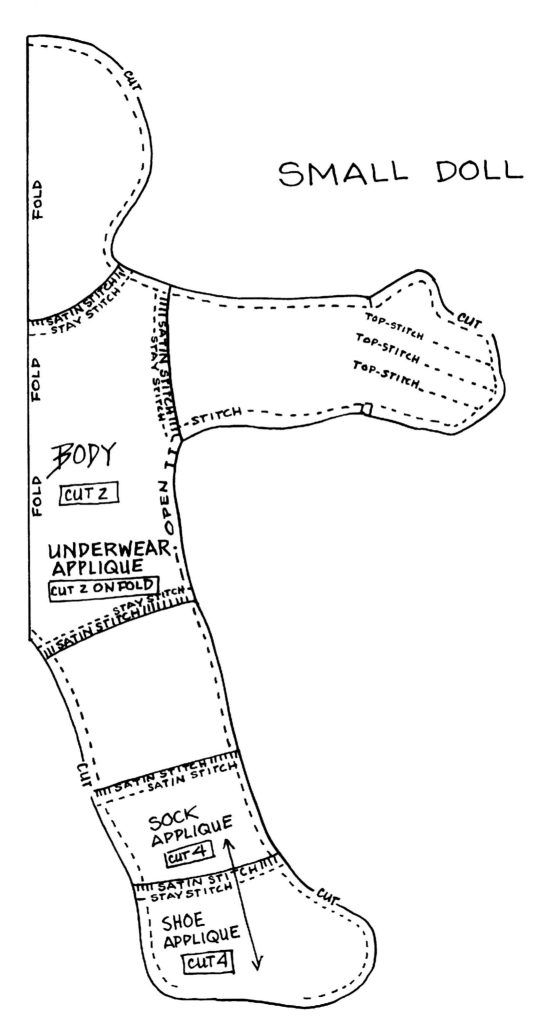

SMALL DOLL

FOLD

CUT

SATIN STITCH
STAY STITCH

FOLD

SATIN STITCH
STAY STITCH

TOP-STITCH
TOP-STITCH
TOP-STITCH

CUT

FOLD

STITCH

BODY
CUT 2

OPEN

UNDERWEAR
APPLIQUE
CUT 2 ON FOLD

STAY STITCH
SATIN STITCH

CUT

SATIN STITCH
SATIN STITCH

SOCK
APPLIQUE
CUT 4

SATIN STITCH
STAY STITCH

CUT

SHOE
APPLIQUE
CUT 4

35

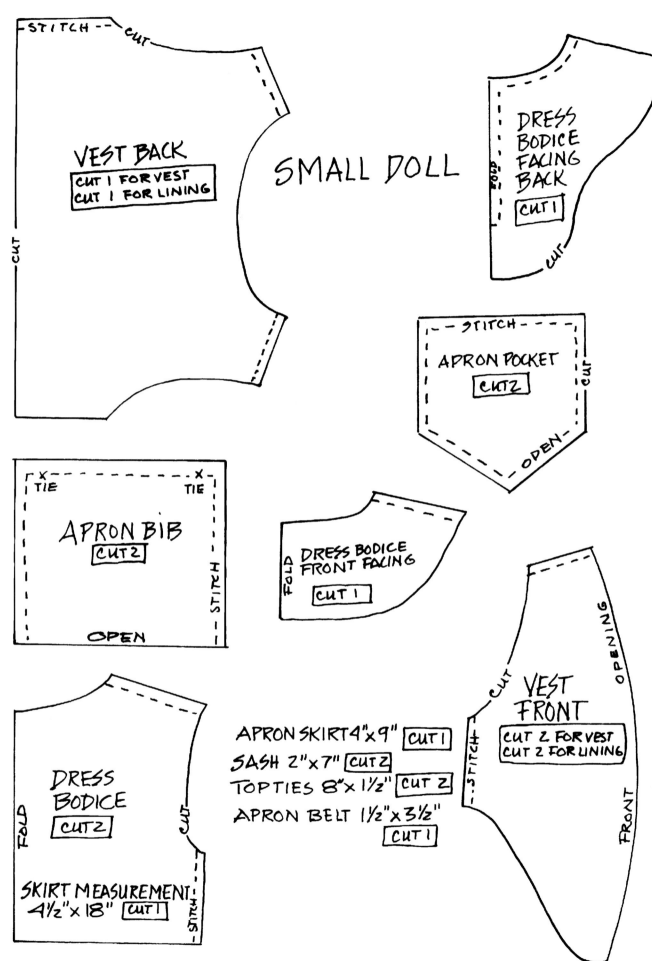

STITCH — CUT

VEST BACK

CUT 1 FOR VEST
CUT 1 FOR LINING

CUT

SMALL DOLL

DRESS
BODICE
FACING
BACK

FOLD

CUT 1

CUT

STITCH

APRON POCKET

CUT 2

CUT

OPEN

X TIE   X TIE

APRON BIB

CUT 2

STITCH

OPEN

FOLD

DRESS BODICE
FRONT FACING

CUT 1

CUT

OPENING

VEST
FRONT

CUT 2 FOR VEST
CUT 2 FOR LINING

STITCH

FRONT

FOLD

DRESS
BODICE

CUT 2

CUT

STITCH

SKIRT MEASUREMENT
4½" x 18"   CUT 1

APRON SKIRT 4" x 9"   CUT 1
SASH 2" x 7"   CUT 2
TOP TIES 8" x 1½"   CUT 2
APRON BELT 1½" x 3½"   CUT 1

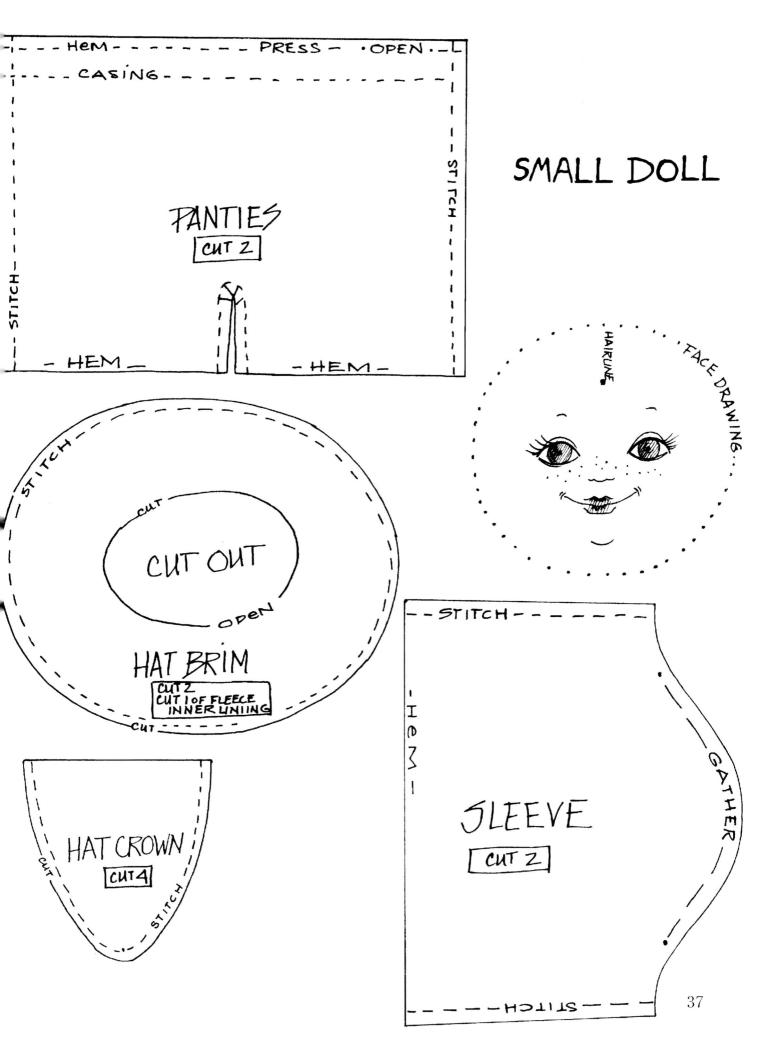

SMALL DOLL

- HEM - - - - - PRESS - - ·OPEN·
- - CASING - - - -

STITCH

PANTIES
CUT 2

STITCH

- HEM -   - HEM -

HAIRLINE

FACE DRAWING

STITCH

CUT

CUT OUT

OPEN

HAT BRIM
CUT 2
CUT 1 OF FLEECE
INNER LINIING

CUT

STITCH

HEM

SLEEVE
CUT 2

GATHER

HAT CROWN
CUT 4

CUT

STITCH

STITCH

37

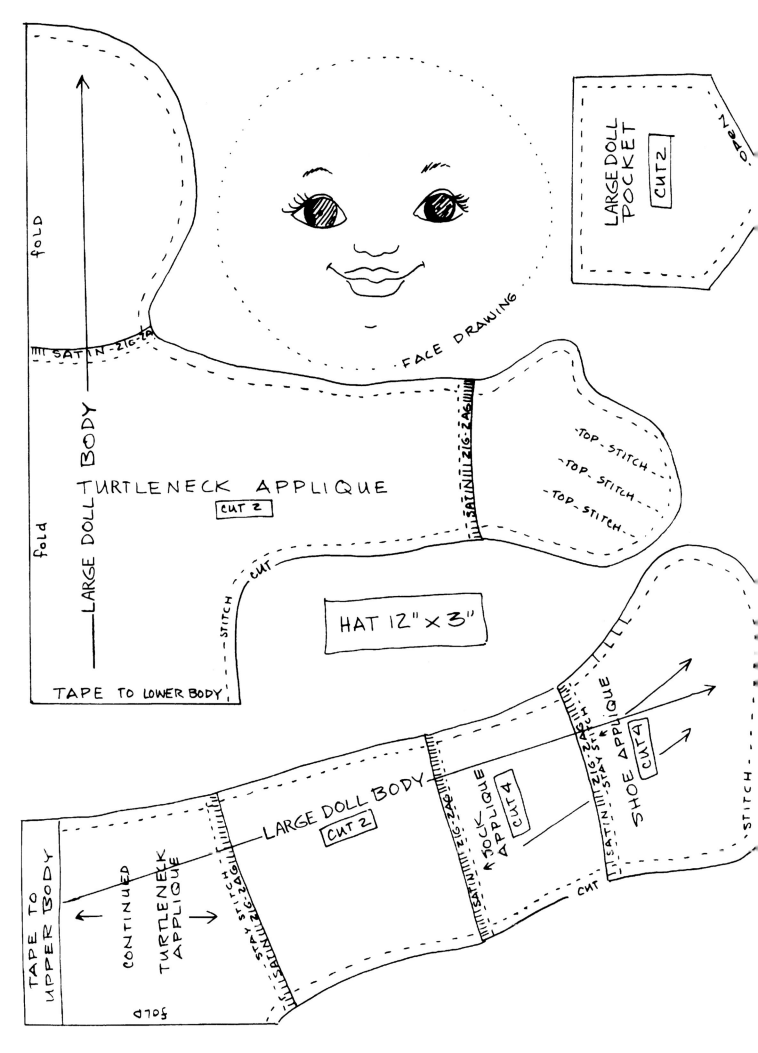

FOLD

SATIN ZIG-ZAG

FACE DRAWING

LARGE DOLL POCKET

CUT 2

OPEN

LARGE DOLL BODY

TURTLENECK APPLIQUE

CUT 2

Fold

SATIN ZIG-ZAG

TOP-STITCH
TOP-STITCH
TOP-STITCH

STITCH

CUT

HAT 12" x 3"

TAPE TO LOWER BODY

TAPE TO UPPER BODY

CONTINUED

TURTLENECK APPLIQUE

STAY STITCH

SATIN ZIG-ZAG

LARGE DOLL BODY

CUT 2

SATIN ZIG-ZAG

STAY STITCH

SOCK APPLIQUE

CUT 4

SATIN STAY STITCH ZIG-ZAG

SHOE APPLIQUE

CUT 4

STITCH

CUT

FOLD

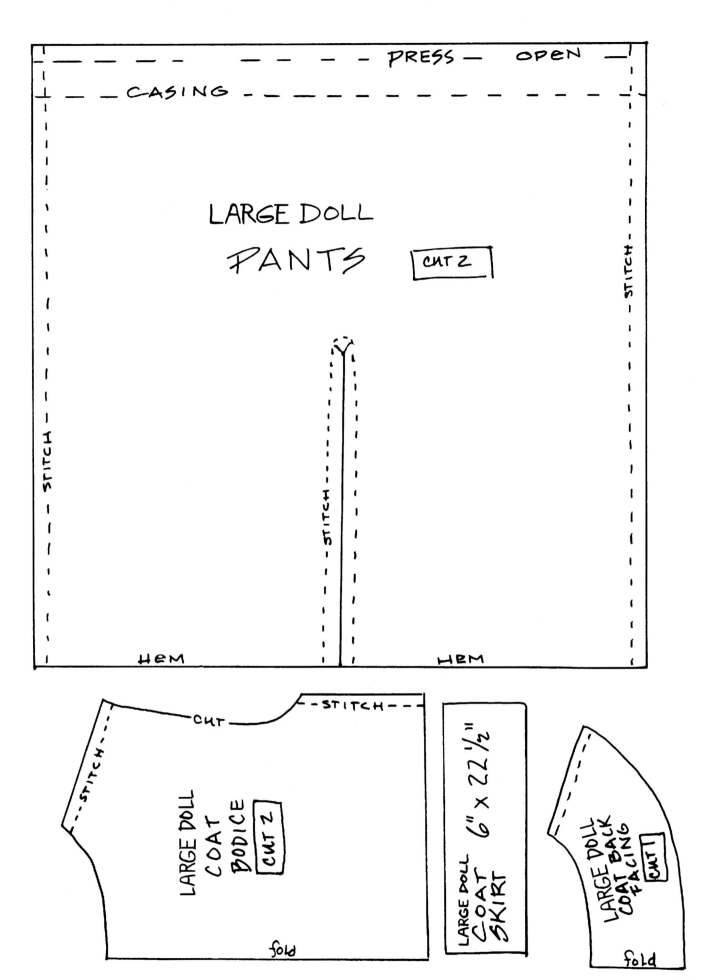

PRESS — OPEN

CASING

STITCH   STITCH

LARGE DOLL
PANTS   CUT 2

STITCH

HEM   HEM

STITCH   CUT   STITCH

STITCH

LARGE DOLL COAT BODICE   CUT 2

fold

LARGE DOLL COAT SKIRT   6" x 22½"

LARGE DOLL BACK COAT FACING   CUT 1

fold

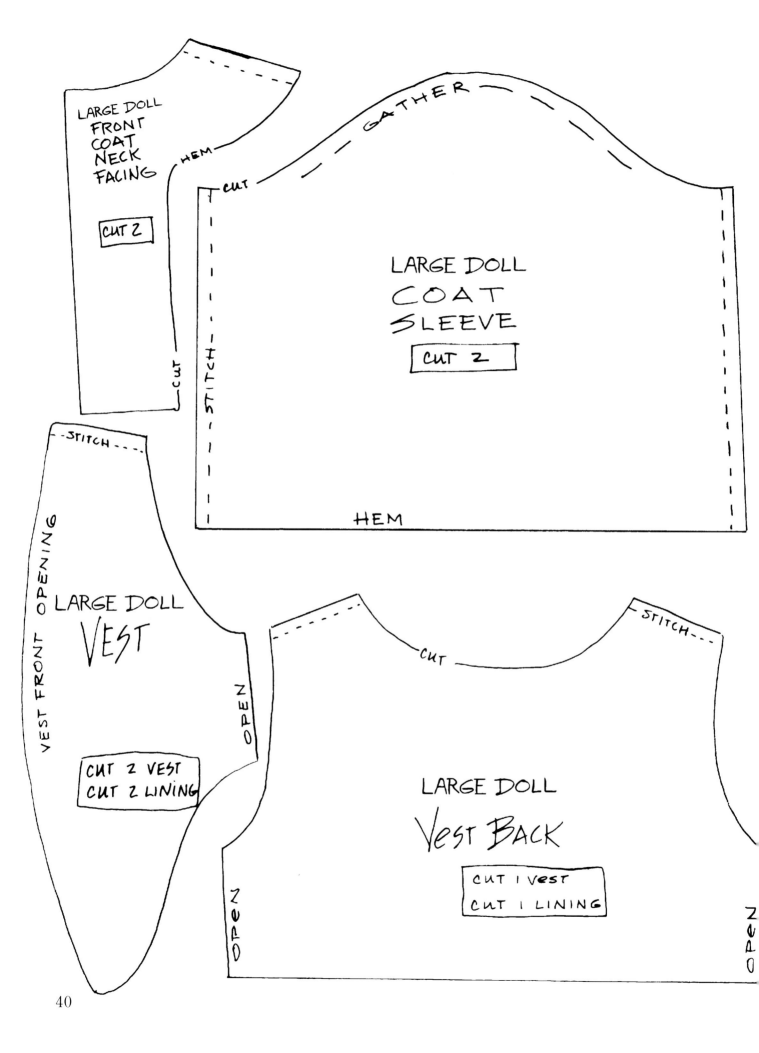

LARGE DOLL
FRONT
COAT
NECK
FACING

CUT 2

HEM

CUT

CUT

STITCH

GATHER

LARGE DOLL
COAT
SLEEVE

CUT 2

HEM

STITCH

LARGE DOLL
VEST

VEST FRONT OPENING

CUT 2 VEST
CUT 2 LINING

OPEN

CUT

STITCH

LARGE DOLL
Vest Back

CUT 1 VEST
CUT 1 LINING

OPEN

OPEN

40

The Longer The Better

The Doll's Story

The dollmaker was pleased. Not bad, she thought, for a simple play doll. Not exactly inspired, of course. The doll is definitely traditional and will not provoke much comment. Okay! The doll is not exciting.

"You're nothing to write home about," said the dollmaker.

"And who's responsible for that?" huffed the doll.

"Well," snapped the dollmaker, "it's not as if you gave me a lot to work with. You're short, and a little chunky."

"Look," replied the doll, "you're the one with all the imagination. You're the one in control. Do something!"

The dollmaker acknowledged that the doll had a point. She gathered patterns, paper and pencil together, and put the doll on a rack. "We're going to stretch you a bit...pull out your legs."

"Oh," groaned the doll. "Enough already."

"Stop complaining. Think of this as a growing experience. Your arms need to come to about here." The dollmaker stood with her arms relaxed at her sides, and observed that her fingertips reached the middle of her thighs. She lengthened the arms of the doll so they would be proportional to the legs.

"Boots," the dollmaker declared. "You need boots. And it's time to make your arms and legs separate from your body."

"Good grief!" the doll shouted. "Will anything about me stay the same? Is nothing sacred?"

"Nothing," replied the dollmaker, who delighted in shocking the doll.

The dollmaker left the head attached to the body, although she altered the body shape a bit and added ears. She decided that ears made the doll look more like a male doll. She imagined he'd need a hat to go with his jaunty bell-bottom trousers and flashy shirt.

The doll peered into the mirror and tried to adjust. "All right! I'm a man. Actually, quite a good looking fellow. Call me Maurice. Or maybe I'll become an African-American and call myself Harry. And you know, if you just used a little more of that imagination you're so proud of, you could make a girl doll out of this pattern as well."

"You think so," ventured the dollmaker.

"Absolutely," responded the doll. "Shape the legs and add a mini-skirt. Make the crown and the brim of the hat a bit larger and then I'd become a girl. Maurice and Harry and the girl could go out dancing. We...I mean the multitude that is I, could have a ball. We could really swing."

"Hey! Quiet down! What do you think this is, anyway?" cautioned the dollmaker.

"Fun! We're having fun!"

The Dollmaker's Workshop

Changing a pancake doll into a jointed doll starts by severing the arms and legs from the body. Observe the proportions: how one part of the body relates to another. This doll is eight heads tall now, and I have made many alterations. The male dolls are entirely dressed when they are finished. The female doll requires only a mini-skirt.

Adding ears to a doll usually makes it appear masculine. If you want to make a female doll with ears, the masculine effect can be overcome by some wild earrings and a feminine hairstyle.

Most of the clothing is appliquéd to the doll, with two exceptions, the hat brim

Changing a pancake doll into a jointed doll starts by severing the arms and legs from the body. Observe the proportions: how one part of the body relates to another.

43

Making up stories to go with your dolls not only adds interest, but may result in a story that comes from deep inside you. You may be surprised by what the doll has to say.

and the shirt. Even the dimensional collar is appliquéd at the neck.

I consider these dolls more decorative than play dolls. They spark up a corner with color and add a touch of humor to a room. These are the kinds of dolls adults like to play with. Part of the play includes making up stories. You may already have invented some stories to go along with your dolls. This not only adds interest but also may result in a story that comes from deep inside you. You may be surprised by what the doll has to say.

The Doll's Story

"You're sitting here talking about all this while I'm laying around being dull and boring," whined the doll. "I mean, I could be out stirring up trouble. Get on with it. I'm ready to be tall and svelte."

"All right, all right," acquiesced the dollmaker. "Let's begin."

The Dollmaker's Workshop

SUPPLIES

Two Boy Dolls And A Girl Doll

- 1/8 yard flesh color for each doll

- 3/8 yard for tights for girl doll

- 3/8 yard for pants for *each* boy doll

- 3/8 yard for arms/sleeves, shirt or blouse, and collar for *each* doll

- 1/4 yard for skirt of girl doll (3/8 yard for striped fabric)

- 1/4 yard for the skirt lining

- Scraps for shoes, necktie and hats

- Scraps of trim for belts and hatbands

- 3" or 5" dollmaker's needle

- Buttonhole twist, crochet string, or waxed linen thread

(more)

44

- Two 1/4" buttons for shoulder joints for each doll

- Buttons for earrings and bolo tie

- Supplies for making faces: pens, crayons, glitter etc.

- Nylon rug yarn for hair for each doll

- Small piece of foam core board (from art supply store)

DESIGN BOARD

If you prop the board next to your work space, you won't spend hours looking for lost pieces.

Making Two Boy Dolls And A Girl Doll

1. Cut the body, ears and hands from selected flesh-colored fabrics. The flesh-colored fabric is your base fabric. All the appliqués are applied to the base body fabric. Remember, people come in many wonderful colors.

2. Cut shirt and blouse appliqués, collars, and arms/sleeves from selected fabrics.

3. Cut pants, pant leg, and boots for the boy dolls, and upper and lower leg tights and shoes for the girl doll, from selected fabrics.

4. Cut pieces of ribbon for the belts on the pants and the skirt.

5. Cut the crowns of the hat and the separate brims. Use the pattern to trace the appliqués so that they will be accurate.

6. Pin the tiny pieces to your foam core design board. If you prop the board next to your work space, you won't spend hours looking for lost pieces.

7. Assemble all the appliqué pieces. Place them on the body parts and secure with a fabric gluestick. Pressing each piece with an iron diffuses the glue. This is a substitute for pinning and basting, but not for stitching.

Remember, people come in many wonderful colors.

45

8. Stay stitch in place, and cover the raw edges with a satin zig-zag stitch.

9. Place the ribbon over the pants of the male doll, both front and back, to form a belt.

10. Top-stitch on both sides of the ribbon at the very edge.

11. Top-stitch two rows of stitching to form a decorative shirt opening.

12. Because the ears are very tiny, you need to make a plastic template from the ear pattern. Draw the ears on a small piece of flesh-colored fabric and stitch slightly within the cutting line. The pattern makes both ears at once.

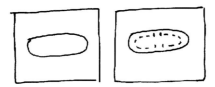

13. After stitching is complete, cut out the two ears. They look like tiny ovals.

14. Cut the ovals in half, and turn each half.

15. Tack the ears in place so they fit in the seam. The placement is indicated on the pattern.

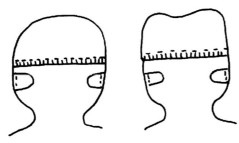

16. With right sides together, stitch the collar, leaving an opening on the short side. Make one stitch across the tip of the collar. Turn and press.

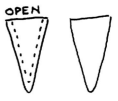

17. Place the two collars on the neck at the top of the shirt and stay-stitch in place.

18. Cover the raw edges with a satin zig-zag stitch.

19. With right sides together, stitch the body. Double stitch in order to prevent popping seams when you stuff the doll. Clip, turn and set the body aside.

DIRECTIONS
Making Legs

1. With right sides together, stitch the legs and appliquéd shoes, leaving an opening as indicated on pattern. Clip, turn, and stuff.

2. Fold the doll so that the toes meet the nose. Stitch the legs to front the body so that the front will be caught in the seam.

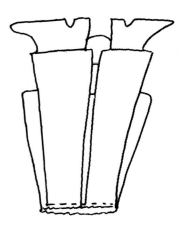

3. Stuff the body. Turn the raw edges in, and place a pin between the legs to keep the opening closed while you stitch. Close the opening by hand with quilting thread, crochet string, or buttonhole twist.

Making Arms

1. With right sides together, stitch arms and appliquéd hands, leaving an opening as indicated on the pattern.

2. Clip, turn, and stuff. Close by hand.

3. Join to the body with buttons. Use a 3" or 5" dollmaker's needle.

4. Using buttonhole twist, crochet string or waxed linen thread, thread a 3" or 5" dollmaker's needle from the inside of the arm, making a knot, to the outside of the arm. Put the needle through the hole in the button, and then back through the second hole, the arm, and the body of the doll.

5. String the second arm in place and add the second button. Return the needle through the second button, through the body, to the first arm. Repeat this process

twice (with waxed linen thread, once is enough).

6. To end this process, bring the needle and thread between arm and button, and wrap a shank. End with a sheep-shank knot. Do this by wrapping a shank between the button and the arm, forming a loop. Pass the needle through the loop, pulling the thread tight, and bury the end of the thread so that you cannot see it.

Making The Hat Brim

1. Cut the brims from the hat fabric and the inner lining from needlepunch batt or fleece.

2. With right sides of fabric together, and batting at the bottom of the lining, stitch around the outer edge. Slash the lining; turn and press.

 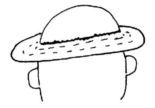

3. Top-stitch concentric circles on the brim to flatten as shown on the pattern.

4. Cut out the center section and slip the brim over the head.

5. Push the raw edges down, and find a 1/4" ribbon for a hatband. Tack the ribbon in place.

Making The Skirt

1. Cut the skirt and lining out of selected fabrics.

2. With right sides together, stitch one side seam of both the lining and the skirt.

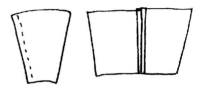

3. With right sides together, stitch together the bottoms or hems of the lining and the skirt.

4. Fold this unit along the stitched side seam as shown, and stitch the remaining side seam. Turn the unit, stuff the lining into the skirt, and press. Fold up the bottom of the skirt to form a cuff.

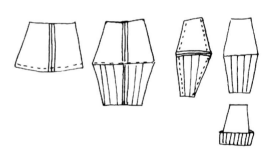

5. Slip the skirt onto the girl doll. Fold in the raw edges at the waist and tack the skirt onto the body. Cover the raw edge with trim for belt.

Making The Face

1. Copy faces onto cloth lightly with a pencil.

2. Draw the features with a fine permanent marking pen.

3. Add color with a brush-tipped fabric pen.

4. Color the cheeks with crayons.

5. Sprinkle a coating of glitter tint to add some fun.

6. For highlights, apply white acrylic tee-shirt paint with a brush.

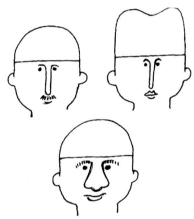

Making Hair

Nylon rug yarn, available at a craft store, usually has three plys. When you untwist it, it frizzes out and creates a full bodied "do."

1. Lay down four or five 6" strands, and tie very tight knots in them.

2. Untwist the ends and trim them.

3. Press the knots in place at each ear under the hat and stitch.

4. Add earring buttons to the girl doll and give her a name.

Making Ties

1. The boy's bolo tie is made with a 3/8" shank button and some pearl cotton thread.

2. The boy's dress tie is made from selected fabric. Stitch with right sides together, leaving an opening to turn with the Bow Whip. Turn.

3. Close the opening by hand, and fold so it looks like a tie.

4. Tack into place by hand, and add a tiny button for a tie-tack.

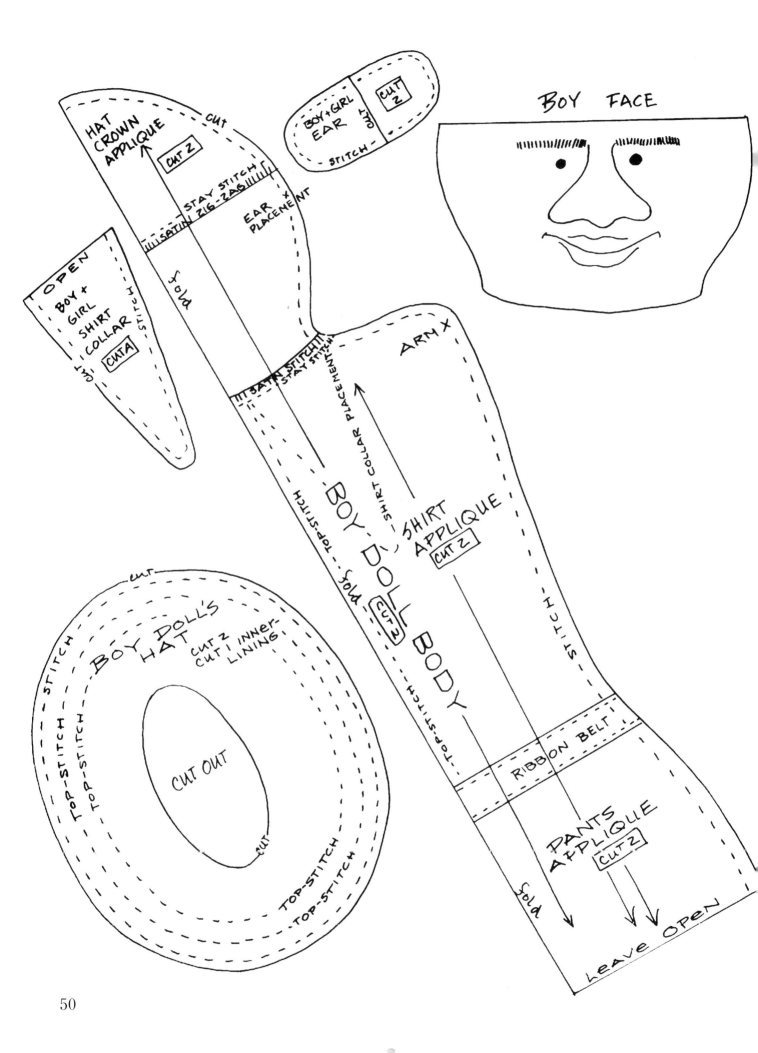

HAT CROWN APPLIQUE
CUT 2

BOY + GIRL EAR
CUT 2

BOY FACE

STAY STITCH
SATIN ZIG-ZAG

EAR X PLACEMENT

Fold

STITCH

OPEN
BOY + GIRL SHIRT COLLAR
CUT 4

SATIN STITCH
STAY STITCH

ARM X

SHIRT COLLAR PLACEMENT

SHIRT APPLIQUE
CUT 2

BOY DOLL BODY
CUT 2

Fold

TOP-STITCH
TOP-STITCH

STITCH

BOY DOLL'S HAT
CUT 2 INNER-LINING
CUT 1

CUT OUT

TOP-STITCH
TOP-STITCH
TOP-STITCH

TOP-STITCH
TOP-STITCH

RIBBON BELT

PANTS APPLIQUE
CUT 2

Fold

LEAVE OPEN

50

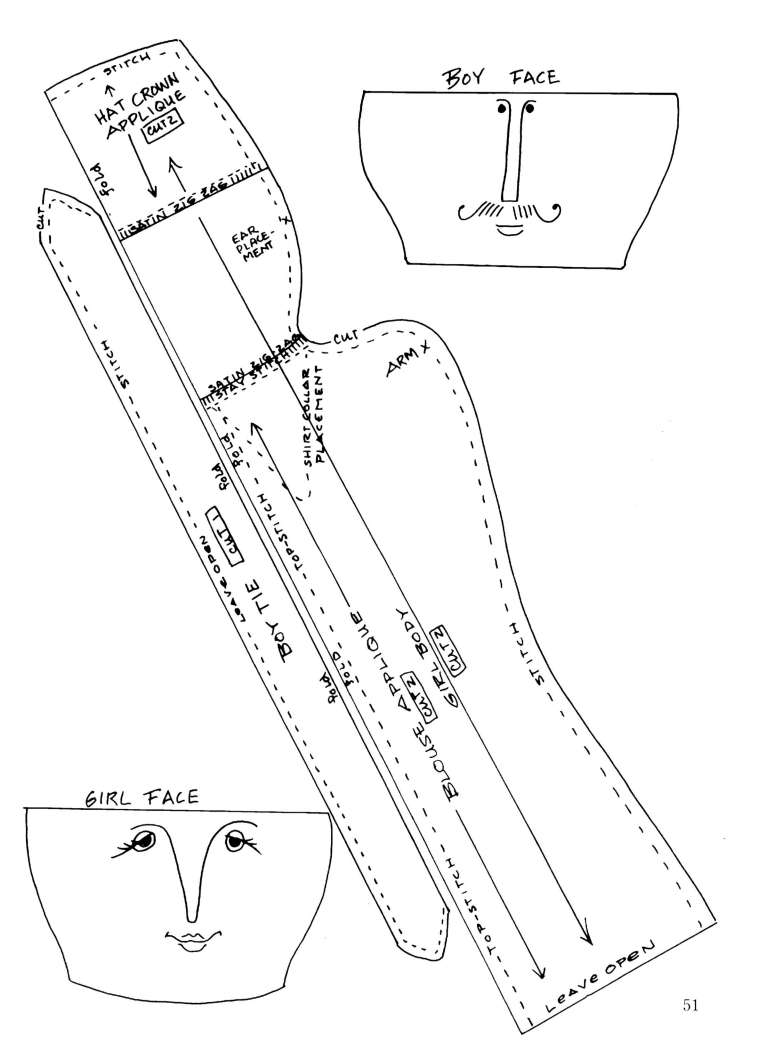

BOY FACE

GIRL FACE

STITCH

HAT CROWN
APPLIQUE
CUT 2

fold

SATIN ZIG ZAG STITCH

EAR
PLACE-
MENT

CUT

STITCH

SATIN ZIGZAG

STAY STITCH

CUT

ARM X

SHIRT COLLAR PLACEMENT

LEAVE OPEN

fold

fold

CUT 1

BOY TIE

TOP-STITCH

fold

APPLIQUE

BLOUSE CUT 2

GIRL BODY CUT 2

STITCH

TOP-STITCH

LEAVE OPEN

51

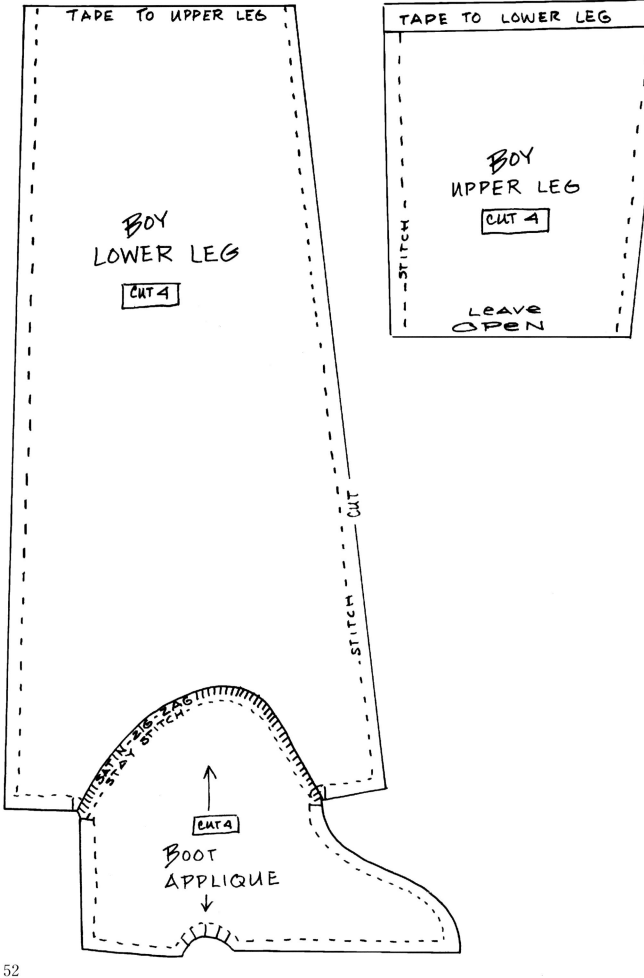

TAPE TO UPPER LEG

TAPE TO LOWER LEG

BOY
LOWER LEG

CUT 4

BOY
UPPER LEG

CUT 4

LEAVE
OPEN

STITCH

STITCH CUT

SATIN ZIG-ZAG
STAY STITCH

CUT 4

BOOT
APPLIQUE

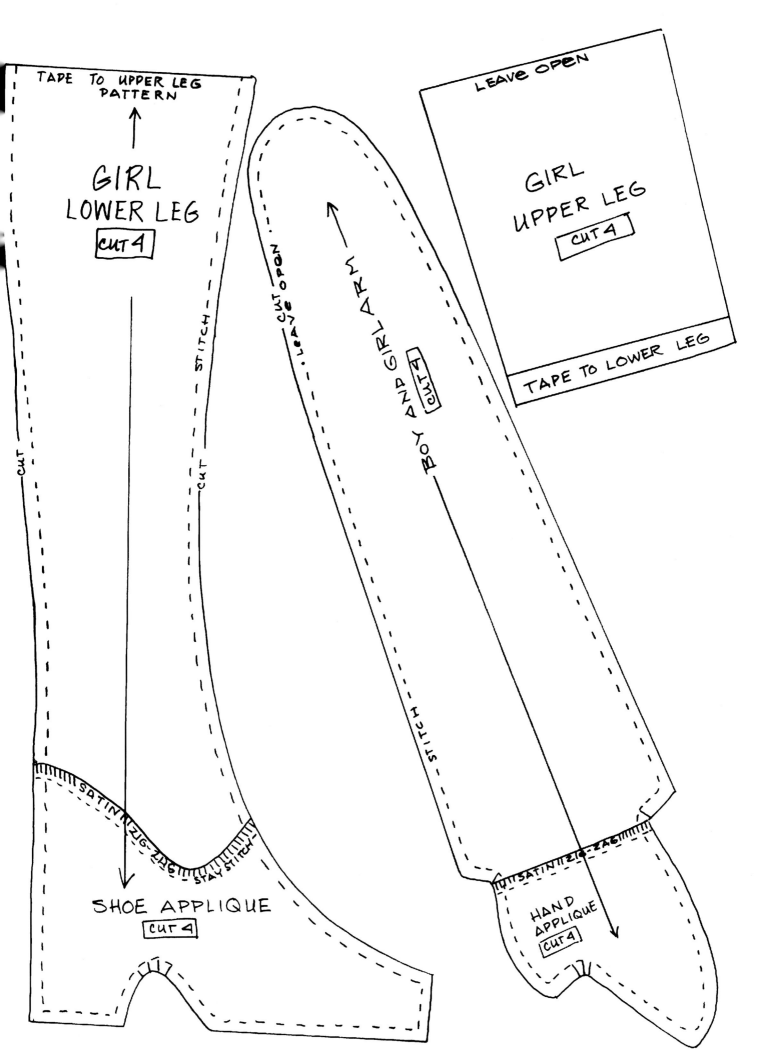

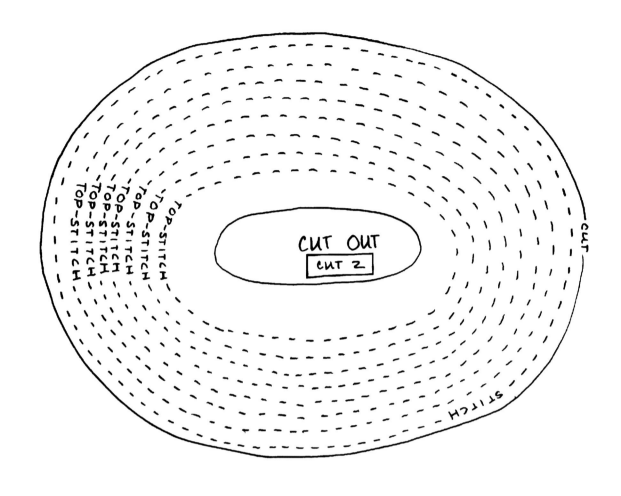

CUT OUT
CUT 2

TOP-STITCH (repeated)

CUT

STITCH

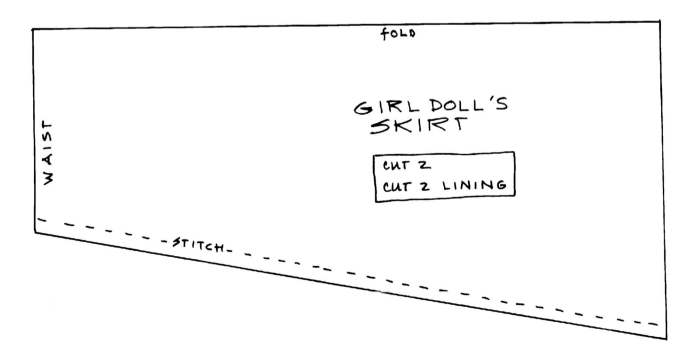

FOLD

WAIST

GIRL DOLL'S
SKIRT

CUT 2
CUT 2 LINING

- STITCH -

Pretty Is As Pretty Does

The Doll's Story

The dollmaker was really pleased with herself. The dolls looked fetching seated on the couch, sociably conversing with one another.

"Well," the dollmaker considered, "where shall we go from here? Actually, I like you just the way you are."

"So do we," chorused the crowd of dolls.

"Although you are still pretty simple," the dollmaker reminded them, "you can't bend at the knee, you know."

The crowd of dolls eyed the dollmaker suspiciously.

"And you can't bend your elbows either," continued the dollmaker. "Your arms hang straight to your bodies...."

"All right, all right!" exclaimed the dolls. "We have our limits. What are you going to do about it?"

The dollmaker fingered her material. She picked up one fabric after another, a stripe, a tiny print, a large romantic floral, a plaid, and back to the floral again. "Hmmm. Sometimes fabrics lead to ideas about a doll, or they suggest a mood or a feeling." She stroked the floral lovingly

while some memories drifted across her face. The dolls watched, fascinated.

First the fabric; then the fantasy. The dollmaker began to sketch a puppet who became a young girl with curls and puffy sleeves, who could sit and bend at the knees and elbows.

"Ahh," the dolls sighed. "Very pretty."

"Yes," agreed the dollmaker happily, and she began.

The Dollmaker's Workshop

Thus far we have looked at the stitched joint, which requires a simple stitch line across the limb, and also at the joint where the limb is severed and then re-joined. We've done button joints at the shoulder where the limb is completely separated and joined with a button.

There are many other joints. Some are inspired by antique porcelain and leather dolls, and others are taken from wooden dolls and puppets. Teddy bears have joints that are metal and need to be buried in their fur.

The joint I am using here is a simple darted joint that I learned from Sally Lampi, a fine dollmaker and a good friend. Because dolls, particularly cloth dolls, come from the art of the folk, their construction is based on ideas often passed between friends like you and me, and then passed on again to others. Each passing is accompanied by changes and alterations, until the doll becomes a reflection of its maker.

In this case, Sally and I discovered that if you sew up a tube of fabric, and then sew across the stitch line at the top of the tube,

Sometimes fabrics lead to ideas about a doll, or they suggest a mood or a feeling.

Dolls come from the art of the folk, based on ideas passed among friends, then passed on to others until the doll becomes a reflection of its maker.

it will flatten the tube. Look at the following illustration to see how the tube looks when it is turned.

When the toes are turned, the bottoms of the feet are flat, and the toes of the shoes are graduated.

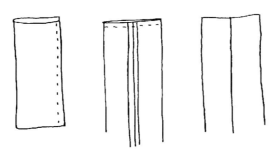

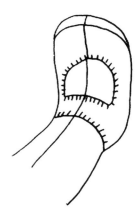

This trick is used to make the foot and the joint on the *pretty doll*. On the *small doll* with pigtails, and on her big sister, feet are made simply by drawing them. I'm going to make a foot that looks like this:

With the joint at the knee and elbow, this process creates a shape like this:

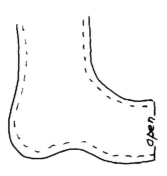

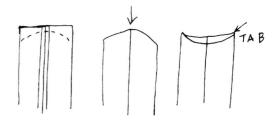

Before turning the foot, I'll sew across the toe and slant the stitch line toward the large toe like this:

Press the fabric down where the two seams meet, and stitch across the little tabs. Then press one tab to one side of the upper leg, and one tab to the other side, and form a hinged joint that reminds me of a wooden puppet.

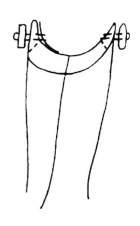

Then I discovered that if I changed the second stitch line, and made a hump, the tabs can be larger.

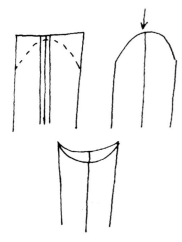

All of the constructions thus far have a head that is attached to the body. If the head is lopped off, then it needs to be larger. I like a slightly oval shape so that the doll can have big romantic eyes to go with the large floral print. To re-attach the head to the body, I created a tab on the body, a sort of post that forms the neck. If the tab is long and slender, it needs a craft stick (which looks like a popsicle stick) to support it. This becomes a form of armature.

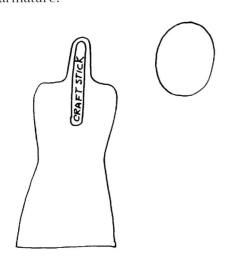

When I designed the head, I decided that I wanted a chin, so I drew a gusset. *Gusset* is a sewing term for anything that expands a shape, while *dart* is a term for anything that contracts a shape. The chin gusset for this doll is shaped like a slug. Right!

To design a gusset, match the center of the gusset to the chin of the doll head, and measure from the bottom where the ear would be on the face to the other side of the face. Then make a slug shape to fit in there. Leave 1/4" free at each tip of the gusset to form a seam allowance when the gusset is stitched to the back of the head. You can do this!

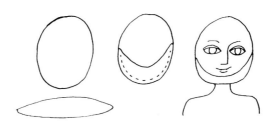

The back of the head is stitched to the front unit, leaving a basted opening to insert the neck tab. The basting thread is clipped and the head is turned from that opening. Now we have a chin.

In order for the doll to sit firmly, a gusset is needed at the bottom. To make this gusset, the body is stitched, leaving an opening at the bottom. After turning, stuff out the edges at the bottom of the body so that it takes the shape you want it to take.

Place the body on a piece of paper and draw around it, adding 1/4" for a seam allowance. This gives you a pattern for the gusset. Slick! Use this pattern to cut out a shape the same color as the body or the underwear. This piece is stitched onto the back side of the body, so that you can put the legs at the front side of the body.

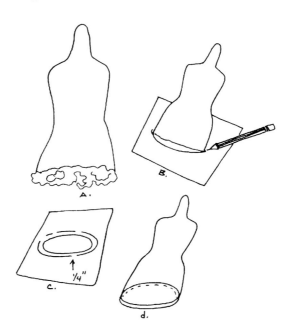

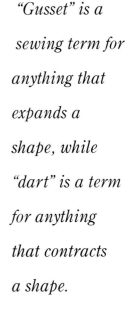

"Gusset" is a sewing term for anything that expands a shape, while "dart" is a term for anything that contracts a shape.

59

The doll as you can see has evolved from a simple pancake shape to a jointed puppet-type doll with a gussetted chin, separated head and gussetted bottom. Let's begin working with these changes.

Pretty Doll

Fantasy flesh colors are endless; explore the possibilities.

- 1/4 yard flesh-colored fabric for head and arms
- 5/8 yard of large, pretty floral for body/dress, skirt and sleeves
- 1/2 yard for petticoat and ruffle
- 1/8 yard for belt
- Scraps for shoes
- 1/4 yard for legs/tights
- 3" or 5" dollmaker's needle and heavy thread
- Eight 3/8" buttons for joints
- Two 5/8" buttons for shoulder joints
- 1/2 yard ribbon, 1-1/2" wide, for hairbow
- 1-1/4 yard lace to trim skirt
- Scrap of lace for neck
- Craft stick and sticky craft glue
- Two buttons for earrings
- Fine-tipped permanent marking pen in brown
- Brush-tipped fabric pens
- Crayola crayons, box of 64
- Dizzle Tints
- Nylon curls by "One and Only Creations"
- White tee-shirt paint

Making The Head

1. Cut two heads and one chin gusset from flesh-colored fabric. Choose flesh color from peaches, pinks, tans, red-browns, browns and blacks. Fantasy flesh colors are endless; explore the possibilities.

2. Find the center of the chin and the center of the chin gusset. With right sides together, match the centers and walk the fabric with your fingers to where the tip of the gusset and the spot under the ear meet. Begin at that point to stitch the gusset to the face.

3. With right sides together, stitch the front of the face unit and the back of the head together. Begin stitching at the top

of the gusset. Stitch over the top of the head into the chin gusset, about 1/2" from the center of the gusset. Back-stitch, baste for one inch, and back-stitch again. Continue stitching until the head is completely enclosed. Clip the basting threads to make an opening for turning.

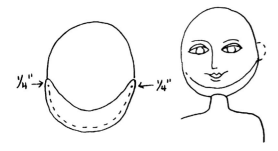

4. Turn the head with the Bow Whip, and stuff the head.

5. Begin painting the face by copying it very lightly with a pencil. Use a fine-tipped permanent marking pen to go over the pencil lines.

6. Select the eye color from brush-tipped pens. I use a light blue and a light violet. Bring color outside the eye to make a shadow. Use a light hand; you can always make it darker.

7. To highlight or to make the eyes white, use a regular opaque tee-shirt craft paint.

8. If you are working with a darker flesh tone, use crayons for blocking in the features. Dark blue makes good lines. Opaque tee-shirt paints show up well on the darker colors.

9. Color the cheeks with crayons. Use brush-tipped pens for the mouth. Apply light colors first, and use dark colors sparingly. Although crayons will not rub out, they will fade a bit, so you can refresh the face from time to time. Add transparent glitter tints to cheeks and eyes. The glitter should be exceedingly fine.

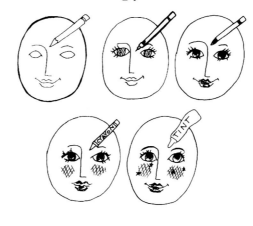

DIRECTIONS
Making The Body

1. Cut the body and the body gusset from the fabric selected from the dress. Find something pretty. This doll loves pretty! Because the doll is made from the dress fabric, the doll is dressed when she is made.

2. With right sides together, stitch the body. Turn the body over and place another row of stitching on top of the first row to secure the seams. Clip and turn.

3. With right sides together, divide the gusset in half. Stitch the gusset to the opening at the bottom of the doll body. The gusset is stitched to the back of the body of the doll.

Find something pretty. This doll loves pretty!

61

DIRECTIONS
Making The Legs

1. Cut out upper and lower legs from a solid color suitable for tights.

2. With right sides together, stitch the upper leg or thigh, leaving the flat side open to turn.

3. Turn and stuff firmly. Press the seams together and stitch across the top.

4. Cut out appliqués for shoes from a scrap of polished cotton.

5. Place the shoe appliqué over the foot of the lower leg and use the fabric gluestick to secure it. Stay-stitch in place. Satin-stitch to cover the raw edges.

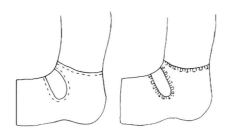

6. With right sides together, stitch the lower leg. Leave openings at the toe, the top of the leg, and the side of the leg.

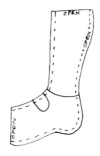

7. Press seams at the toe together. Stitch a half-moon across the top of the toe to form the toe of the shoe.

8. Press seams at the top of the leg together to make the joint tabs. Stitch a half-moon. Trim the toe and joint, and turn.

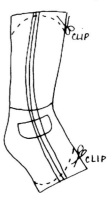

9. Stitch joint tabs and stuff firmly. Close the opening carefully by hand.

10. Stitch the tabs around the upper joint, using two 3/8" buttons, a 3" dollmaker's needle, and heavy thread (quilting or waxed linen thread, crochet string or buttonhole twist).

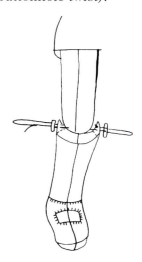

11. Make a knot between the tab and the knee. Bring thread through the tab to the outside. Pass needle and thread through the buttonhole. Bring the needle and thread back through the button, tab, knee, tab and button. Repeat to secure. Bring the needle out behind the button and wrap the thread to form a shank. Make a loop and pass the needle through it. Pull tight and bury the thread. When you make the elbow joint, you will repeat this process.

12. Stuff the body, filling the neck first. Be very assertive. Put some craft glue on the end of a craft stick (popsicle stick) and slide it to the back of the neck. Stuff the remainder of the doll firmly. Give her some backbone! You might want to place a bean-bag filled with plastic pellets inside the bottom for added weight.

13. Tack the top of the legs in place at the front of the body. Flip the bottom gusset over the top of the legs. Use one pin to hold the gusset in place. Close the opening by hand with heavy thread.

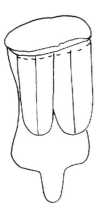

14. Use your finger to drill a hole in the head of the doll, at the place where the head will receive the body neck tabs. Stitch the head in place by hand with quilting thread.

Making The Arms

1. Cut the upper and lower arms from flesh-colored fabric. Cut the sleeves from dress fabric.

2. With right sides together, stitch the upper arm, leaving an opening to turn. Stuff and close by hand with tiny overcast stitches.

3. With right sides together, stitch the hand and the lower arm, leaving openings at the top and on the side, as indicated on the pattern. Make smaller stitches for the fingers. Do this carefully.

4. Place two stitches across the web of the finger so that you can clip right to the stitch line. Use Stop-Fraying to secure the stitching. Before the hand dries, clip to the stitch line. Turn the fingers with the Bow Whip, using the smallest tube.

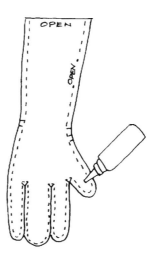

5. Stuff fingers with tiny pieces of Polyfil. Top-stitch the middle fingers by machine in order to divide them.

63

6. To make the elbow joint, follow the instructions for the knee.

7. With right sides together, stitch the sleeves, leaving open on the straight side. Clip, turn and hem the bottom edge by hand.

8. Slip the sleeve over the top of the arm. Use a 5" dollmaker's needle, heavy thread, and two 5/8" buttons to secure the arm in place. Go back and forth three times, wrapping around the button (between sleeve and button) to form a shank. Bury the thread and clip.

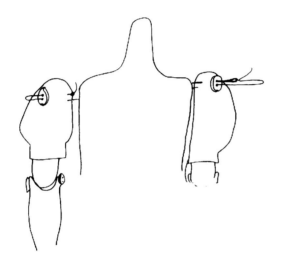

DIRECTIONS
Making The Skirt

1. Cut 15" x 45" skirt from pretty floral. Cut 10-1/2" x 45" petticoat and two 2-1/2" x 45" strips for the ruffle from a complementary fabric.

2. With right sides together, stitch the two ruffle pieces together lengthwise. Hem the bottom edges. Add lace or a fancy stitch if you like.

3. Gather the top of the ruffle and even out the gathers. Fit the gathers to the petticoat and pin in place.

4. Stitch the ruffle to the petticoat. Press the seam up, and top-stitch the seam to flatten the edges.

5. With right sides together, press up a 3" hem on the bottom of the skirt to form a facing for the scallop edges of the skirt.

6. Match the center of the skirt to the center of the scallop pattern. There are nine scallops, one in the center and four on each side. Draw around the scallop, joining one scallop to another. This becomes the stitching line. Stitch along the line, trim to 1/4" and clip thoroughly. Turn and press.

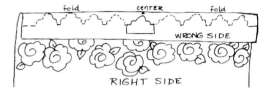

7. Stitch the facing of the scallop to the skirt. Sew trim on top of the stitch line to cover it.

8. Place the skirt on top of the petticoat. The petticoat ruffle should peak from beneath the skirt. If the length is wrong, trim at the top to make it even. Using a 3" dollmaker's needle and heavy thread, gather the skirt *by hand* to fit around the doll's waist. Distribute the gathers and zig-zag by machine to keep in place.

9. Cut the 4-1/2" x 45" belt from contrasting fabric. With right sides together, match the center of the belt to the center of the skirt and petticoat at the waist. Stitch the skirt to the belt.

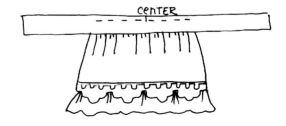

10. With right sides together, fold the belt and stitch across the belt to the waist. Turn from opening at the waist. Press and tack by hand at the back of the waistband.

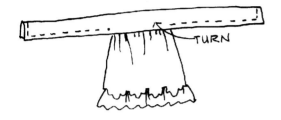

11. Machine-stitch the side of each skirt individually to 1-1/2" below the waist. Slip onto the doll.

12. With the doll's head facing toward you, tie a glorious bow.

The Doll's Story

The doll looked into the mirror and frowned. "This would be a perfect picture except for one thing. I'm bald!"

"Well," said the dollmaker, "what shall it be?"

"Curls," simpered the doll. "I absolutely must have curls."

The dollmaker found a bag of nylon curls she had purchased at a craft shop. The curls sprang out of the bag like so many Slinkies. She stitched them in place with a quilting needle.

The doll voiced her approval, and began to make further demands. "Now I need some lace around my throat, and earrings and roses at the breast please." She insisted on an ostentatious one-half yard to place on her head. She minced before the mirror, primping and showing off, until she made the dollmaker perfectly ill.

The doll twirled her skirt and refused to do a lick of work. Her demands to be waited on and catered to exhausted the dollmaker, who did not like being ordered about. She was dismayed at being nearly broke from buying presents like hats, fans, purses and even a special chair for a doll who displayed the attitude of a princess.

The curls sprang out of the bag like so many Slinkies.

65

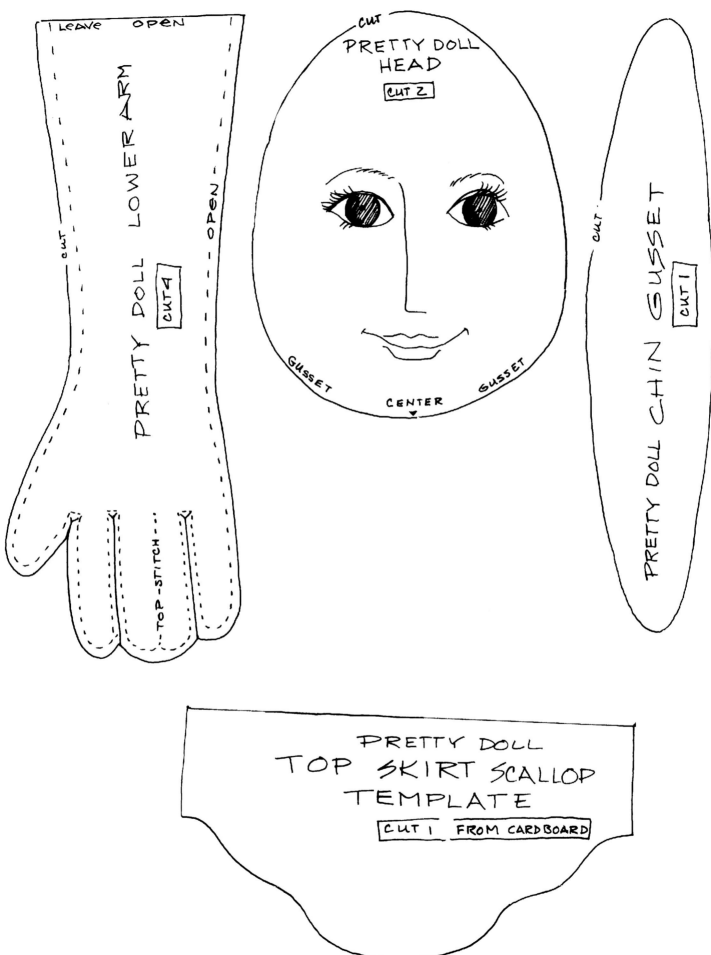

LEAVE OPEN

PRETTY DOLL LOWER ARM

CUT

OPEN

CUT 4

TOP-STITCH

CUT

PRETTY DOLL
HEAD

CUT 2

GUSSET

CENTER

GUSSET

CUT

PRETTY DOLL CHIN GUSSET

CUT 1

PRETTY DOLL
TOP SKIRT SCALLOP
TEMPLATE

CUT 1 FROM CARDBOARD

66

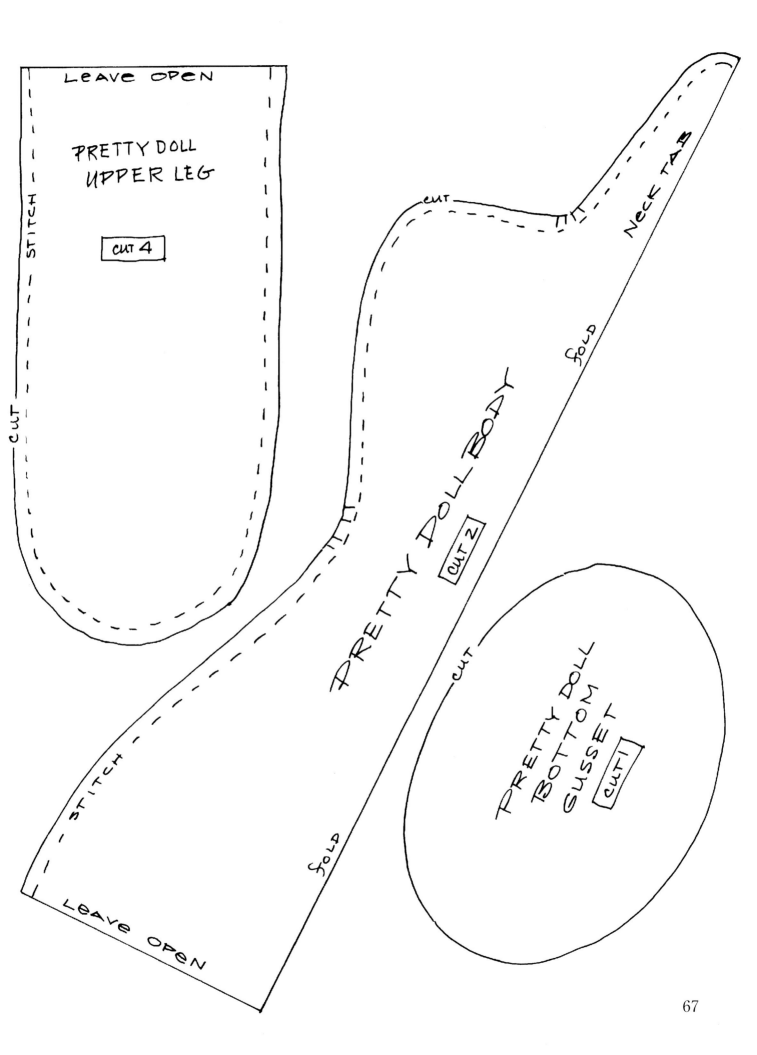

LEAVE OPEN

PRETTY DOLL
UPPER LEG

CUT 4

STITCH

CUT

STITCH

LEAVE OPEN

PRETTY DOLL BODY

CUT 2

CUT

FOLD

FOLD

NECK TAB

PRETTY DOLL
BOTTOM
GUSSET

CUT 1

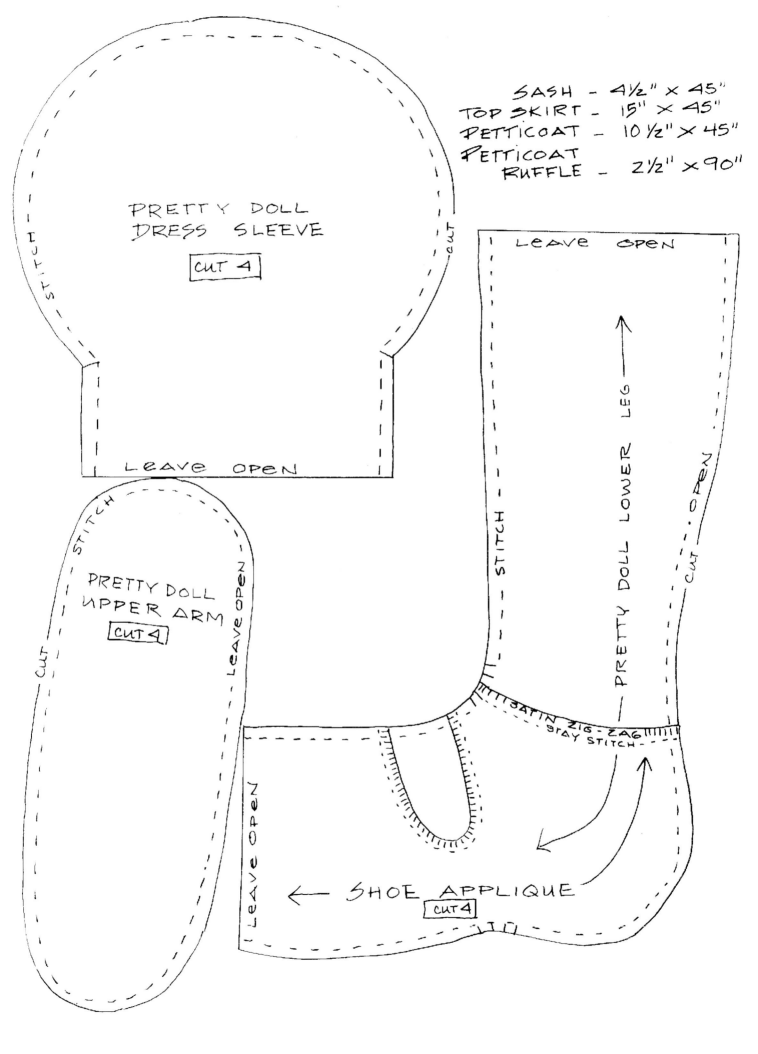

PRETTY DOLL
DRESS SLEEVE

CUT 4

STITCH

CUT

LEAVE OPEN

PRETTY DOLL
UPPER ARM

CUT 4

STITCH

LEAVE OPEN

CUT

LEAVE OPEN

SASH – 4½" × 45"
TOP SKIRT – 15" × 45"
PETTICOAT – 10½" × 45"
PETTICOAT
RUFFLE – 2½" × 90"

LEAVE OPEN

STITCH

PRETTY DOLL LOWER LEG

CUT OPEN

SATIN ZIG-ZAG
STAY STITCH

LEAVE OPEN

← SHOE APPLIQUE

CUT 4

Me, Myself And I

The Doll's Story

One day, after a particularly trying conflict, the dollmaker retreated to her studio and furiously began to draw a new pattern.

"Whatever are you doing?" asked the doll in an imperial voice.

"Another doll," snapped the dollmaker, for she had lost patience.

"Why bother," whined the doll. "Who could be more wonderful than me?"

"We shall see," replied the dollmaker, who continued her project undeterred by the doll's obvious disapproval. First she constructed a face, not flat like the other faces were, but with dimension and character. She gave the doll's body broader dimensions and some womanly curves. She added articulated thumbs, breasts, a jacket, a hat and a full skirt. She made sensible shoes for the doll's feet.

The pretty doll stared in amazement. She saw that the new doll taking shape in the hands of the dollmaker began to reflect the dollmaker herself.

This is how it has always been. We begin at the beginning, simple and uncomplicated, but in the end we are always left staring back at ourselves. Isn't it wonderful that in the end the creator is mirrored in her creations, and that you can see yourself in what you make?

The Dollmaker's Workshop

The process of creating a profile on a doll is very simple. The challenge is to keep the front of the face the same circumference as the back of the head, no matter what changes are made. In other words, the distance around the head must remain the same regardless of how the features are altered. Let's use the same head that was used for the pretty doll to discover how this works.

DIRECTIONS
Creating A Profile

1. Fold the head pattern in half from top to chin. Press the fold into a crease.

2. Unfold the head, and draw a nose and a bit of a curve for a mouth.

3. Add 1/4" seam allowance, beginning at the forehead or top of the head and continuing to the chin.

4. Use this pattern to cut two profiles from flesh-colored fabric. Place right sides together and stitch.

5. The head is finished with a gusset in the same way as the Pretty Doll.

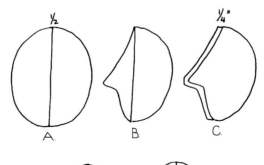

Isn't it wonderful that in the end the creator is mirrored in her creations, and that you can see yourself in what you make?

71

Adding Shape To The Body

Observation is the key to reshaping the body by adding some curves. I have myself as a model, and you must find your own.

Observation is the key to reshaping the body by adding some curves. I have myself as a model, and you must find your own. She may be as handy as your looking glass. To keep the scale the same, place tracing paper over the pretty doll pattern and trace. If the body is nude, then the breasts can be applied to match the body. I have used a clothed body, adding breasts in the same color as the doll's shirt.

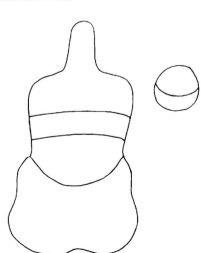

1. To apply underwear to the naked body, place a band of underwear fabric across the doll's chest.

2. Add half-moons of underwear fabric on the breasts, so that you create the illusion of a bra.

3. I like to dart the doll's breasts to give them more shape. I mean, I have my vanity to consider. Make these darts by following this diagram:

4. Use a slug-shaped gusset to make another body change. This time the gusset is narrower at the crotch and wider at the buttocks. To minimize the guesswork with the bottom gusset, measure from the side where underwear would come (if there were some) to the other side, and make the slug shape about that size. There will be an opening on the back of the doll's body for stuffing. Trial and error will prove to be your best friend.

5. Notice the change in the drawing of the lower arms, where the joint tabs are a little larger so that the arms come away from the body.

6. The upper arm is stitched to the shoulder, with the tab running down the body like an armpit. The remainder of the arm is folded down over the tab so that it can hang slightly away from the body.

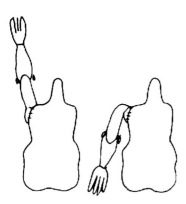

7. The legs are attached at the pelvis. It is not possible to hinge the upper thigh to this body because of the curves. Attaching the legs at the pelvis means that this doll is permanently seated. On many days that is a happy thought for me.

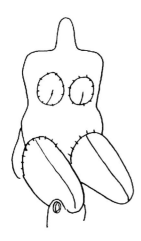

8. Enlarging the thighs is an exercise in realism. Turn the thighs so that the seams are facing up and down instead of across.

9. To make an articulated thumb, cut off the thumb and then re-join it. Dollmakers need nimble fingers. Re-attaching the thumb requires the same pressing of one shape to another that all appliqué shapes require.

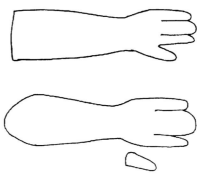

10. Everything stays the same in the shaping of the foot and leg, but the dollmaker wears high-top tennis shoes. This illusion is created with a cuff that fits around the shoe appliqué, and the addition of a shoe tongue. Make the cuff from a paper pattern that fits around the ankle, adding a 1/4" seam allowance.

If you made these changes, you can make others. You go from simple to complex, from plain to fancy. The final place is out there where neither you nor I have ever been. What is most important is that you find yourself in the dolls. A doll may remain very simple and accomplish just that. But knowing how to add detail and dimension gives you more opportunities to put your individual stamp on your creations.

You go from plain to fancy. The final place is out there where neither you nor I have ever been.

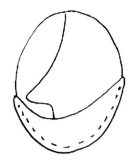

The Dollmaker Doll

What is most important is that you find yourself in the dolls.

- 1/8 yard flesh-colored fabric for head and hands
- 1/2 yard for turtleneck and tights for body, arms and legs
- 1/8 yard for hat
- 1/8 yard polished cotton for shoe appliqué, cuff and tongue
- 1/2 yard each for jacket and lining
- 1/2 yard for skirt
- 1/4 yard thin batting for inner-lining of jacket
- 3" dollmaker's needle
- 7" yarn darner needle
- 8 shirt collar buttons for arm and leg joints and buttons for earrings
- Quilting thread to match flesh-colored fabric
- Craft stick and sticky craft glue
- Mini-dolls for jacket
- Necklace made from a beaded earring
- Pearl cotton for shoelaces
- Face painting supplies

DIRECTIONS

Making The Head

1. Cut the four-piece doll's head from a piece of flesh-colored fabric, adding a scant 1/4" seam allowance. This time, make her the same color as yourself.

2. With right sides together, stitch the profile. Diminish the 1/4" seam allowance to 1/8" as you stitch carefully around the nose. Return to a scant 1/4" at the chin.

3. Add the chin gusset. With right sides together, center the gusset to the seam and stitch, leaving 1/4" open at each of the two tips of the gusset.

4. Stitch the back of the head to the front unit, beginning at the tip of the gusset.

5. Fold the gusset back and stitch over the top of the head to the other side of the gusset, leaving an opening at the center back of the gusset to receive the neck tab. Back-stitch, baste and back-stitch again.

6. Remove the basting stitches and turn. Stuff firmly.

7. Add some needle sculpture with a 3" dollmaker's needle and quilting thread that matches the skin color. Enter the head at the top, using a knot to anchor. The knot will be covered with hair.

8. Bring the needle out where the corner of the eye meets the bridge of the nose, and take a tiny stitch to form a loop. Bring the needle and thread through the loop and draw it tight. Bring the needle back through, very close but not into that stitch, to the other side of the bridge of the nose. Go back and forth and pull slightly to make the desired indentation. Do this three times.

9. Enter at the eye, bringing the needle out at the opposite nostril under the nose, and return. Go back to the remaining eye indentation and down to the opposite nostril until it looks right. Bring the

needle to the top of the head and tie off the thread. If this whole thing is looking kind of witchy, check the firmness of the stuffing. It must be firm.

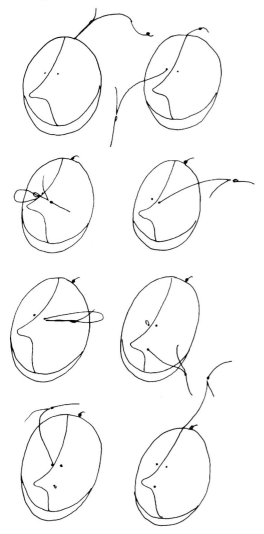

10. Draw the face by copying it lightly, using a pencil to make minimal lines. Use a fine-tipped permanent marking pen to make the final line drawing.

11. Color the eyes with a brush-tipped fabric-marking pen and crayons. Shade the eyes with soft color. Soft can always be made darker.

12. Make the eyeglasses the color you've always wanted. If she's too young or too vain for glasses, then eliminate them.

13. Using brush-tipped pens, give the mouth two colors. Try red and orange, or magenta and fuschia.

14. Rouge the cheeks with crayon, and finish with sparkling tints.

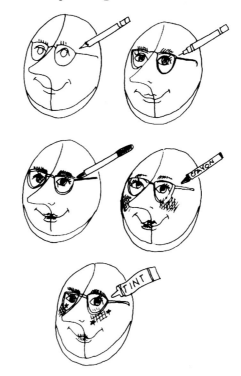

DIRECTIONS
Making The Body

1. Cut the body, body gusset, breasts, arms and turtleneck from selected fabrics. The doll will be dressed when it is stuffed, and will appear to be wearing a turtleneck jersey.

2. With right sides together, pin the gusset to the body front. You choose which side is front. Match the narrow part of the gusset to the crotch of the body. Stitch in place, leaving 1/4" open at the tip of the gusset. Stitch again, forming a double-stitch.

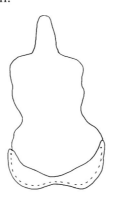

Knowing how to add detail and dimension gives you more opportunities to put your individual stamp on your creations.

3. With right sides together, stitch the body, leaving an opening on the gusset so that you can stuff the doll from the bottom. Back-stitch, baste, and back-stitch to keep the gusset from stretching. Again, double-stitch. Clip and open the basting stitches to turn the body.

4. Stuff the neck firmly. Insert a craft stick with some tacky glue at the back of the stuffed neck for support. Continue stuffing around the neck and finish stuffing the body. Give this woman some backbone! Close the body opening by hand with small overcast stitches.

5. Stitch the darts on the breast. Trim and gather around the breast by hand, using quilting thread and a sharp needle. Knot the thread to anchor. Pull the gathers and stuff the breast full, leaving a space at the back of the breast about the size of a nickel. Tie off the thread. Press the breast to the body until it forms a ridge, and tack in place with tiny back-stitches.

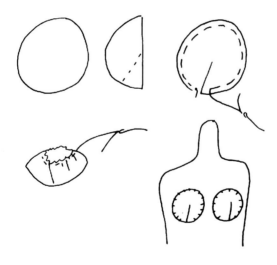

DIRECTIONS
Making Legs

1. Cut the thigh, lower leg, shoe appliqué and tongue from selected fabrics. My doll is wearing tights which I made the same color as her shirt, but you have choices here.

2. With right sides together, stitch the thighs, leaving an opening at the top. Turn and stuff firmly.

3. Use a sharp needle and matching quilting thread to make gathers around the top of the thigh. Pull the gathers. Press the thigh into the body and tack in place with tiny back-stitches.

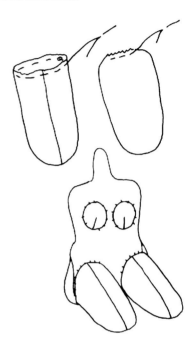

4. Use fabric glue to hold the shoe appliqué in place on the lower leg. Stay-stitch 1/8" from the edge at the ankle. Cover the raw edges with a satin zig-zag stitch.

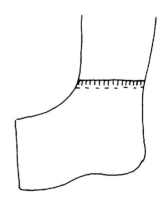

5. With right sides together, stitch the lower leg, leaving openings at the top, side and toe. Press the two seams together at the top and stitch the joint tabs.

6. Press the seams together at the toe by stitching a half-moon shape to form a rise at the large toe.

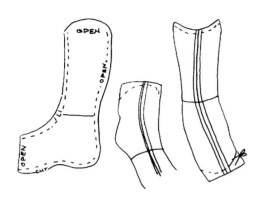

7. Trim, clip and turn from the opening at the back of the lower leg. Press down the rise at the top of the lower leg to form two tabs for the joint, and stitch across the tabs. Stuff the remainder of the leg firmly and close by hand.

8. Join the lower leg to the thigh, using two shirt collar buttons, a #7 darning needle and quilting thread. Put a knot between the tab and the knee, bringing the needle through the tab and then through the buttonhole. Return the needle through the buttonhole, the tab and the knee to the second tab and another button. Repeat the process three times. Then wrap the thread in back of one of the buttons to form a shank. Make a loop, pull the thread through the loop, pull tight, and bury the needle. Repeat for the other leg.

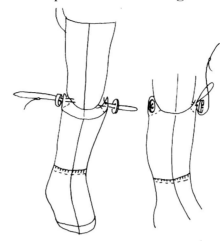

9. With right sides together, stitch the high-top tennis shoes, cuffs and tongues. Leave open where indicated on the pattern. Turn with the Bow Whip, stuff lightly, and close by hand. To trim, use a contrasting thread. Stitch 1/8" from the edge with a zig-zag satin stitch.

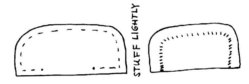

10. Wrap the cuff around the top of the high-top tennies and tack in place. Tuck the tongue in where the sides of the cuff meet. Tack in place.

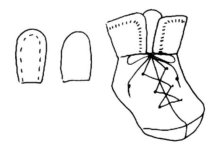

DIRECTIONS
Making Arms

1. Cut out the upper arms, lower arms, and appliqués for hands and thumbs from fabrics selected for turtleneck and flesh.

2. With right sides together, stitch the upper arm, leaving open just below the underarm tab stitch line. Turn with the Bow Whip and stuff the tab lightly.

3. Top-stitch to form a stitched joint as indicated on the pattern. Stuff the remainder of the arm firmly and close the opening by hand.

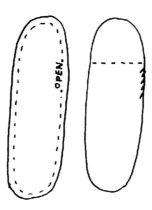

4. Attach the upper arm to the body by placing the underarm tab downward at the shoulder. Stitch in place. Attach across the shoulder as well. The upper arm folds over itself at the stitch line, so that the arm comes slightly away from the body.

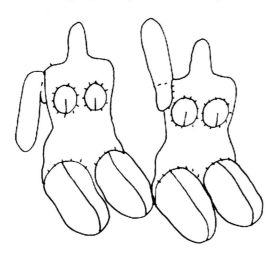

5. Put the hand appliqué in place with a fabric gluestick. Stay stitch at the wrist. Use matching thread to cover the raw edges with a satin-stitch. Because the fingers are narrow, I suggest that you cut away the fabric from behind the hand appliqué.

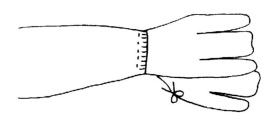

6. With right sides together, stitch the lower arm and hand, leaving openings at the top and side of the arm. Use a 1.5 stitch length to make two stitches across the web of the two outside fingers.

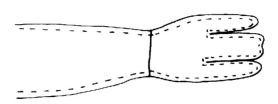

7. Use Stop Fraying to secure the stitching. Carefully clip the two outside fingers to the stitch line. If wrinkles form at the web of the fingers when they are turned with the Bow Whip, you were not courageous enough.

8. Press the seams together at the top of the arm. Stitch the joint tabs. Clip. Turn from the opening on the side of the arm.

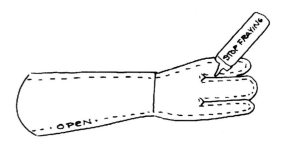

9. Use the smallest tube on the Bow Whip to press the tube against the tip of the finger, creating a receptacle for the metal dowel. Pull the fabric back over the dowel. Do not push the dowel. Pull the fabric. Complete turning the finger, and then

78

turn the whole arm. Whee! Go get some chocolate.

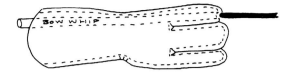

10. Stuff the two center fingers lightly, and machine top-stitch the separation between the two fingers. Stuff the remaining finger.

11. Depress the stitch at the top of the arm to create the joint tabs. Stitch across the tabs. Stuff the remainder of the arm and close the opening by hand. Attach the upper and lower arm using the method for the upper and lower leg.

12. With right sides together, stitch the thumb, leaving an opening to turn. Turn and stuff. With a sharp needle and matching quilting thread, make gathers around the open end of the thumb. Pull the gathers until the raw edges fold in. Press the thumb in place on the hand until it looks natural. Tack in place with tiny stitches.

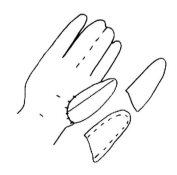

DIRECTIONS

Attaching The Head, Hair And Hat

1. With right sides together, stitch the two short sides of the turtleneck into a tube. Turn the tube and place it around the neck, hiding the raw edges so that it looks like a turtleneck shirt.

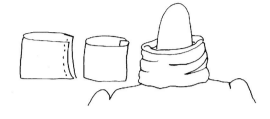

2. Drill a hole in the head with your finger so that the head can receive the neck tab. Twist the head in place to give the doll an attitude. Stitch the head in place with quilting thread.

3. There are many choices for hair. I've used four-ply nylon rug yarn. Begin wrapping the rug yarn around the 4" width of a 4" x 6" piece of cardboard. Continue until the card is covered with 6" of wrapping. Slide the yarn off the card and stitch it down the center, creating a fringe. Cut the fringe and stitch across the top of the head by hand.

4. The hat covers the rest of the head. Cut the hat from jaunty fabric.

5. With right sides together, stitch the long sides of the lining and the hat.

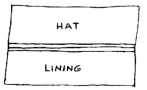

Whee! Go get some chocolate.

79

6. With right sides together, make a tube of the lining and the hat along the seamed edge.

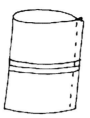

Now is the time to use your imagination.

7. With right sides together, stitch the crown to the hat. Stitch the crown lining to the hat lining, leaving an opening at the lining. Turn, and stuff the lining into the hat. Press.

8. Mount the head at a cocky angle, and add some earrings for effect. Now is the time to use your imagination.

DIRECTIONS
Making The Skirt

1. Find that spiffy fabric you selected for the skirt. Cut two pieces, one 6" x 22-1/2" and one 11" x 45."

2. Gather the 11" x 45" piece to fit the 22-1/2" side of the other piece. Pin in place and, with right sides together, stitch the two pieces into two tiers.

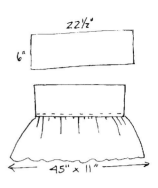

3. Fold down 1/2" to make a casing for 1/4" elastic waistband, and press in place. Press under a tiny hem. Top-stitch, leaving a small opening for threading the elastic into the casing.

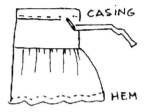

4. Measure the 1/4" elastic around the waist of the doll. Thread the elastic into the casing, using a safety pin to guide it. Join both ends of elastic to form a waistband and tack to hold.

5. Hem the bottom of the skirt and put it on the doll.

DIRECTIONS
Making The Jacket

1. Cut the jacket and lining from the selected fabric, placing them on the fold at center, front and back. Both the jacket and the lining are each made from one piece of fabric.

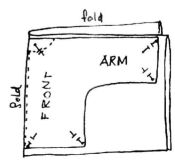

2. Cut an inner lining of batting from the same pattern.

3. Place the inner lining of batting on the back of the jacket top. Pin, baste or quilt the layers together so that they do not slip.

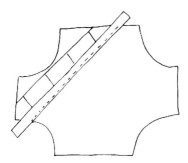

4. If you wish, you can piece the jacket like I did. Just do some fancy work with strips of fabrics and squares until you make a piece that is big enough. Cut the jacket out of the resulting "fabric."

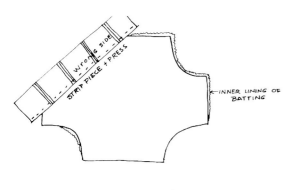

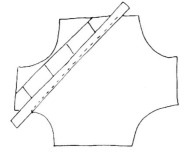

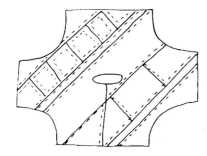

5. Slash the jacket, the lining and the batting at the center front.

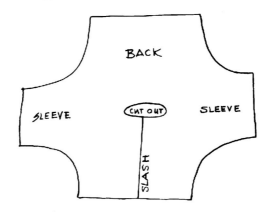

6. Fold at the shoulder and, with right sides together, stitch under the sleeves. Repeat for the lining.

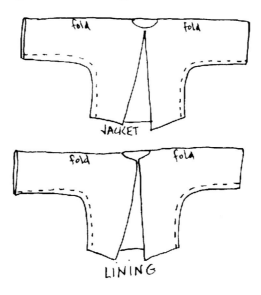

7. Place the lining and the jacket, right sides together, at the front opening of the jacket. Pin in place and stitch around the opening, leaving an opening at the jacket bottom to turn. Clip, turn and press. Topstitch if necessary.

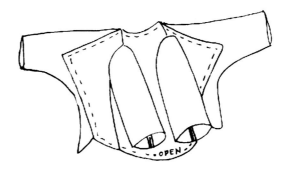

8. Stuff the lining into the jacket. Hem the sleeve on both the jacket and the lining, and hand-stitch to finish the edge.

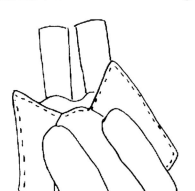

Look in the mirror, and remember that the goal is to have the dolls reflect who you are.

9. Now it's time to drag out all those inexpensive trinkets you've been saving, like Guatemalan worry dolls and those neat Columbian dolls. Maybe you need to go shopping. Inexpensive earrings are another resource. If all else fails, make some tiny dolls for her to wear.

There she is. Look in the mirror, and remember that the goal is to have the dolls reflect who you are. We came into this world to be ourselves and no one else. As the poet said, "I am me, for that I came."

Bring her things to make things with. She needs the tools of her trade. Keep her happy.

82

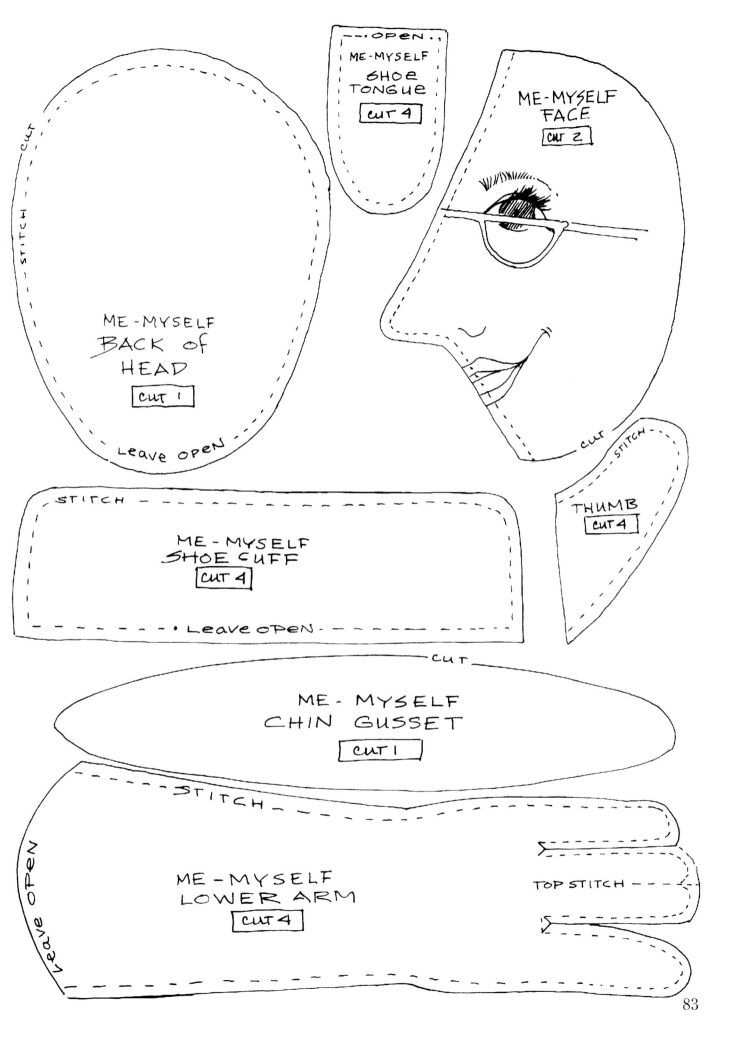

OPEN

ME-MYSELF
SHOE
TONGUE

CUT 4

ME-MYSELF
FACE

CUT 2

CUT

STITCH

ME-MYSELF
BACK OF
HEAD

CUT 1

LEAVE OPEN

CUT

STITCH

THUMB

CUT 4

STITCH

ME-MYSELF
SHOE CUFF

CUT 4

LEAVE OPEN

CUT

ME-MYSELF
CHIN GUSSET

CUT 1

STITCH

LEAVE OPEN

ME-MYSELF
LOWER ARM

CUT 4

TOP STITCH

83

LARGE DOLL TURTLENECK 3" x 7"

CUT
STITCH
ME-MYSELF
BODY
CUT 2
LEAVE OPEN AT BACK

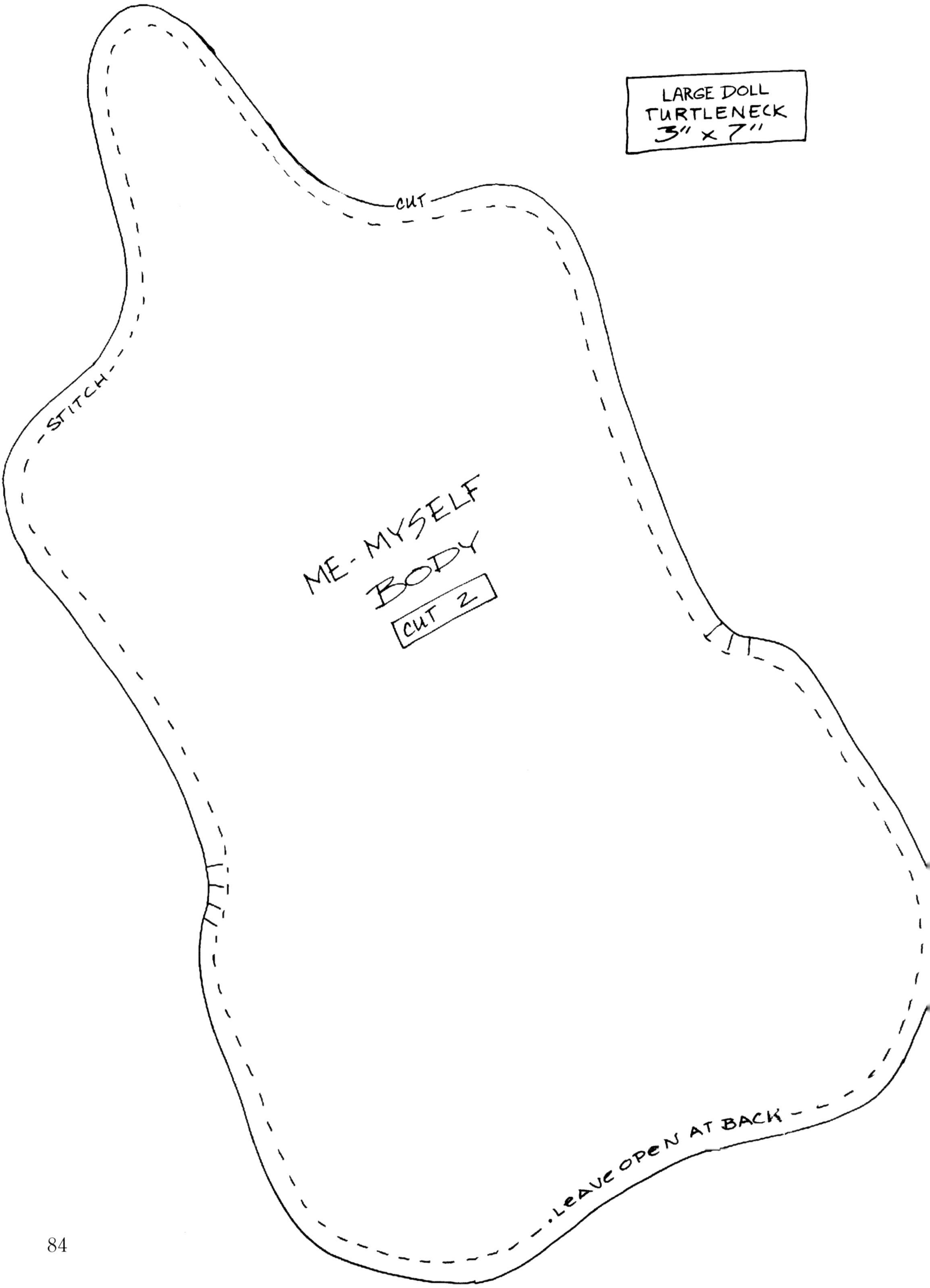

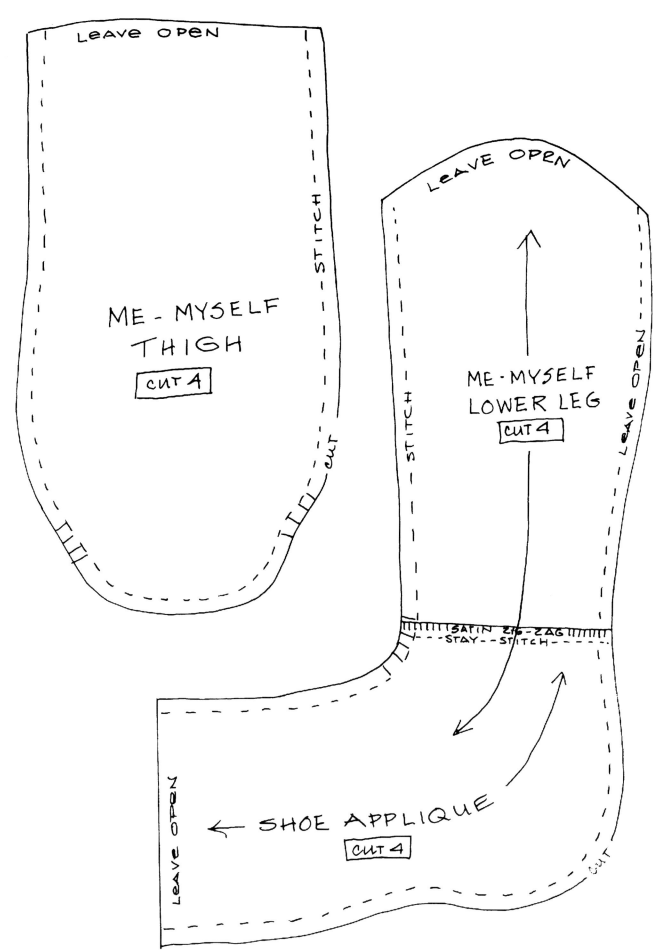

LEAVE OPEN

STITCH

ME - MYSELF
THIGH
CUT 4

CUT

LEAVE OPEN

STITCH

LEAVE OPEN

ME - MYSELF
LOWER LEG
CUT 4

SATIN ZIG-ZAG
STAY - STITCH

LEAVE OPEN

SHOE APPLIQUE
CUT 4

CUT

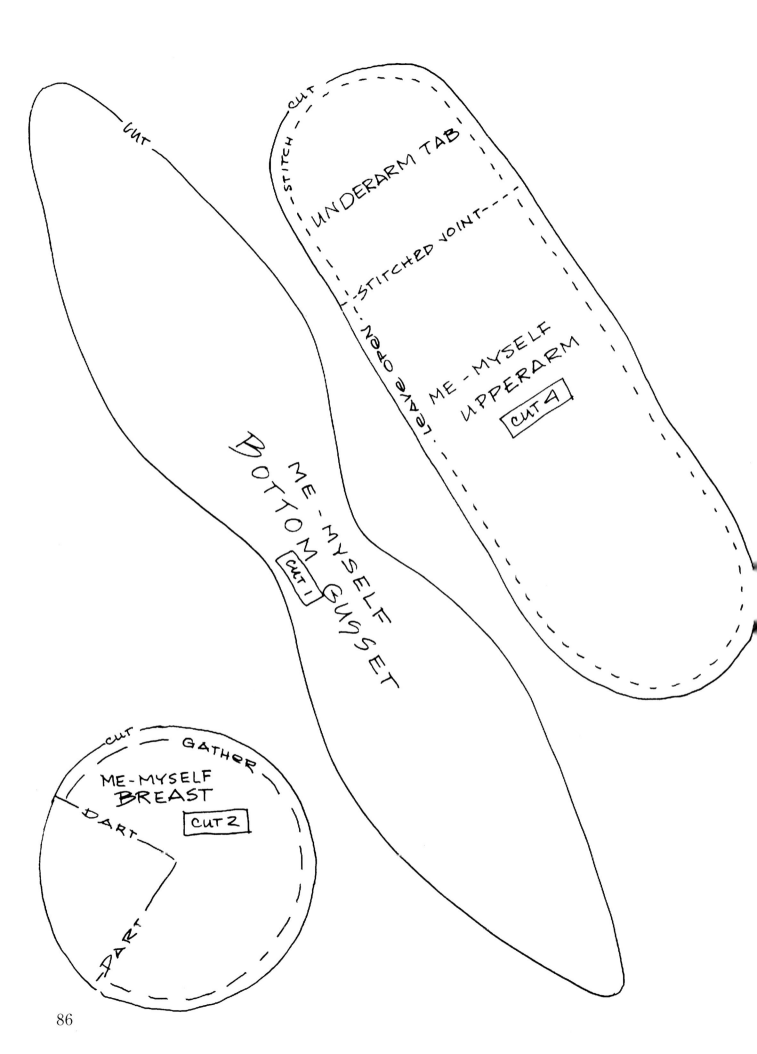

CUT

STITCH CUT

UNDERARM TAB

STITCHED JOINT

ME-MYSELF
UPPERARM

CUT 4

leave open

ME-MYSELF
BOTTOM GUSSET

CUT 1

CUT
GATHER

ME-MYSELF
BREAST

CUT 2

DART

DART

DART

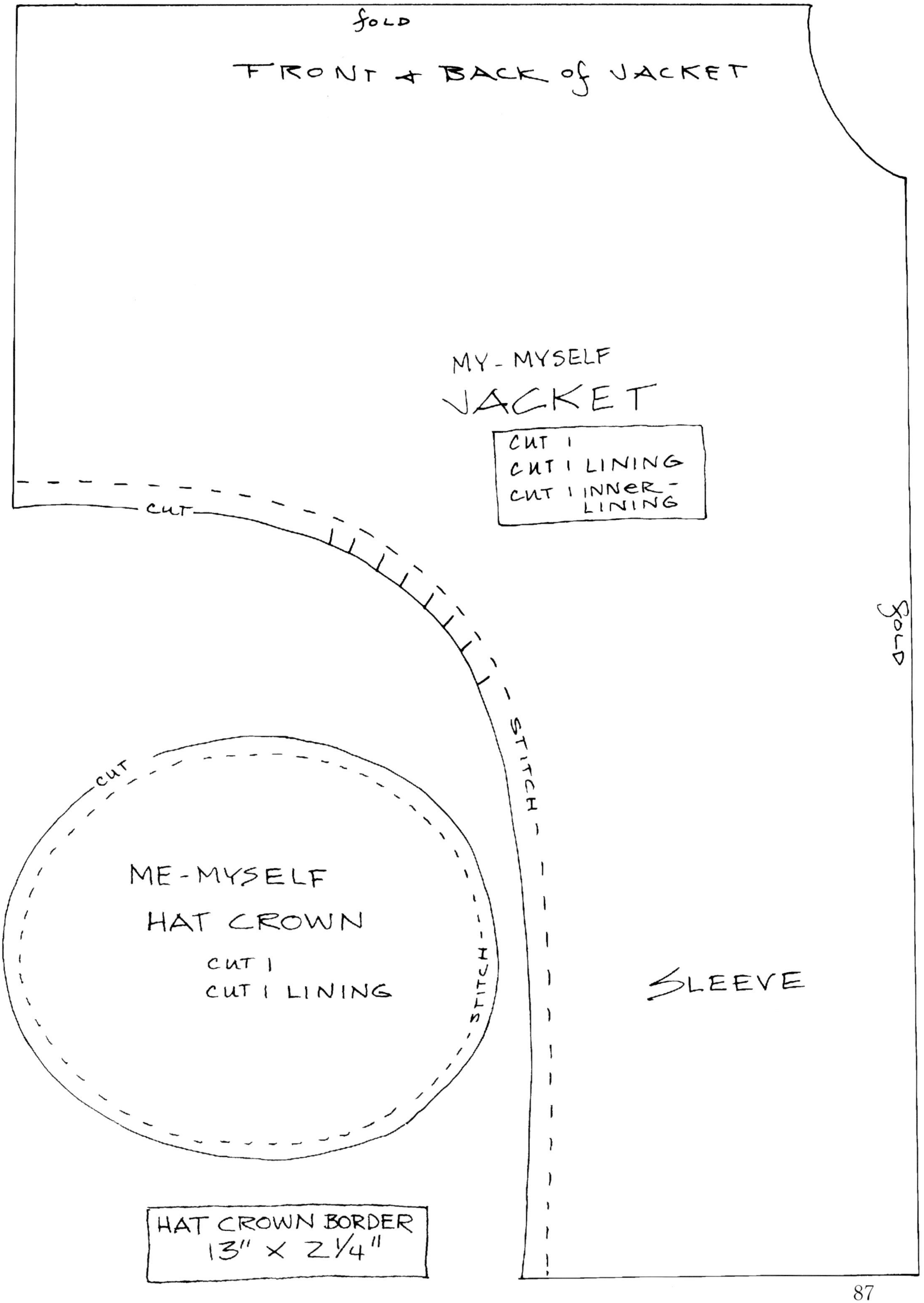

fold

FRONT & BACK of JACKET

MY - MYSELF
JACKET

CUT 1
CUT 1 LINING
CUT 1 INNER-
LINING

CUT

STITCH

fold

CUT

ME - MYSELF
HAT CROWN

CUT 1
CUT 1 LINING

STITCH

STITCH

SLEEVE

HAT CROWN BORDER
13" × 2¼"

The Plain Old Rag Doll

A fractious rag doll
Made of stuffing and cloth
Crawled into my basket and sighed.
Said she, "It seems sad
That a thing such as I
Should be chewed up
And tossed to one side."

"Ah, dollie," said I,
"Your plight I decry.
You are surely a sad sorry sight.
I will sit here and sew
Some dandy new clothes.
I will mend you and give you new life."

Now the doll though restored,
Was just a bit bored.
"Could you manage a bit more pizazz?
I fancy long legs
And a couple of dates,
A night on the town with some jazz."

"I fear you've grown bold,
And I've lost all control,
I must get me some scissors at once.
I shall pick something neat,
That is ever so sweet,
With flowers and ribbons and flounce."

"Oh, lovely" said she,
"A Princess, that's me!
Bring me some presents. I'm just too divine.
Oh, aren't you impressed
With my lovely new dress
And my hair hung in rings
All my charming new things."
"Oh, stop it!" I cried.
I marched out in a huff,

For I'd had enough,
Doll parts were all I could see.
I cut and I drew.
The poly-fil flew.
Now what I'd made was a "me."

For we can pursue
A figure that's new.
We can look for that face by the hour.
But the image we find
That we can't leave behind,
Is the one that we see in the mirror.

How To Organize A Doll Club

It may have occurred to you that joining together with other dollmakers would be fun, and so it is. I have been a member of the Flying Phoebes of Hayward, California for over six years. We have had five doll shows, the most recent featuring seven-hundred and fifty cloth dolls which were displayed in my home.

Dollmakers from all over the country, as well as Australia, New Zealand, Canada and England have formed groups for the purpose of making dolls. Some groups focus on making porcelain dolls, some paper, some cloth and a variety of other media.

Groups facilitate imaginative play. Challenges are exchanged and show and tell is always popular. Sharing tips about faster and easier techniques and tools makes a doll club invaluable. Someone always has a new idea to throw into the pot.

How does one go about starting a doll club? It's easier than you may think. First of all, design a flyer. It should be enough of an attention grabber to make folks curious to pick it up. Your flyer might even feature a drawing that you could use later as a mascot. Select a date that is convenient for you (let's face it: you're going to be president. How else can you get your own way?) Pick a place. Your local quilt shop or sewing store may welcome you, or you could meet in a private home. All you need is three people. That's enough to cause some trouble.

I recommend that you set three goals. The first is to make dolls (none of those "let us entertain you" members). The second is to plan and publish a newsletter, charging sufficient dues to cover the cost. Keeping in touch and offering small patterns created by group members keep the group involved. The third goal is to schedule a show one year from the date of your first meeting, even if you have to hold it in a closet with ten dolls. This motivates the group to get cracking.

Let's make dolls and help to heal the world.

elinor peace bailey

90

The Dollmaker's Library

Bailey, Elinor Peace. *Mother Plays With Dolls*. McLean, Virginia: EPM Publications, Inc., 1990.

"The Cloth Doll Magazine." Portland, Oregon: Beswick Publishing.

"The Contemporary Doll Magazine." Livonia, Michigan: Scott Publications.

"Dollmakers Journal." Austin, Texas: The Firefly Group, Inc.

"Dollmaking Projects and Plans." Iola, Wisconsin: Jones Publications.

Gourley, Miriam. *Cloth Dolls, How To Make Them*. Gualala, California: Quilt Digest Press, 1991.

Gourley, Miriam. *Whimsical Animals, Dolls To Make From Fabric*. Lafayette, California: C & T Publishing, 1993.

*Laury, Jean Ray. *Doll Making, A Creative Approach*. New York, New York: Van Nostrand Reinhold Company, 1970.

McKinley, Robert. *Dollmaking, One Artist's Approach*. Richmond, Virginia: McKinley Books, 1991.

*Meilach, Dona Z. *Soft Sculpture and Other Soft Art Forms*. New York, New York: Crown Publishers, Inc., 1974.

Oroyan, Susanna. *A Collector's Guide, Contemporary Artist Dolls*. Cumberland, Maryland: Hobby House Press, Inc., 1985.

Oroyan, Susanna. *Fantastic Figures, Ideas, and Techniques For The New Clays*. Cumberland, Maryland: Hobby House Press, Inc., 1994.

"People Who Play With Dolls" newsletter. elinor peace bailey, Hayward, CA

Taylor, E.J. *Dollmaking*. New York: Workman Publishing Co., Inc., 1987.

*Wiseman, Adele. *Old Woman At Play*. Toronto/Vancouver Canada: Clarke, Irwin and Company, 1978.

*out of print

Dollmaker's Notes